Embedded and Empowered

PRACTICAL GUIDES FOR LIBRARIANS

About the Series

This innovative series written and edited for librarians by librarians provides authoritative, practical information and guidance on a wide spectrum of library processes and operations.

Books in the series are focused, describing practical and innovative solutions to a problem facing today's librarian and delivering step-by-step guidance for planning, creating, implementing, managing, and evaluating a wide range of services and programs.

The books are aimed at beginning and intermediate librarians needing basic instruction/guidance in a specific subject and at experienced librarians who need to gain knowledge in a new area or guidance in implementing a new program/service.

About the Series Editors

The **Practical Guides for Librarians** series was conceived and edited by M. Sandra Wood, MLS, MBA, AHIP, FMLA, Librarian Emerita, Penn State University Libraries from 2014 to 2017.

M. Sandra Wood was a librarian at the George T. Harrell Library, the Milton S. Hershey Medical Center, College of Medicine, Pennsylvania State University, Hershey, PA, for more than thirty-five years, specializing in reference, educational, and database services. Ms. Wood received an MLS from Indiana University and an MBA from the University of Maryland. She is a fellow of the Medical Library Association and served as a member of MLA's Board of Directors from 1991 to 1995.

Ellyssa Kroski assumed editorial responsibilities for the series beginning in 2017. She is the director of information technology at the New York Law Institute as well as an award-winning editor and author of thirty-six books including *Law Librarianship in the Digital Age*, for which she won the AALL's 2014 Joseph L. Andrews Legal Literature Award. Her ten-book technology series, the Tech Set, won the ALA's Best Book in Library Literature Award in 2011. Ms. Kroski is a librarian, an adjunct faculty member at Drexel and San Jose State University, and an international conference speaker. She has just been named the winner of the 2017 Library Hi Tech Award from the ALA/LITA for her long-term contributions in the area of library and information science technology and its application.

Titles in the Series Edited by M. Sandra Wood

1. *How to Teach: A Practical Guide for Librarians* by Beverley E. Crane
2. *Implementing an Inclusive Staffing Model for Today's Reference Services: A Practical Guide for Librarians* by Julia K. Nims, Paula Storm, and Robert Stevens

Embedded and Empowered

A Practical Guide for Librarians

Courtney Mlinar

PRACTICAL GUIDES FOR LIBRARIANS, NO. 54

ROWMAN & LITTLEFIELD
Lanham • Boulder • New York • London

Published by Rowman & Littlefield
An imprint of The Rowman & Littlefield Publishing Group, Inc.
4501 Forbes Boulevard, Suite 200, Lanham, Maryland 20706
www.rowman.com

6 Tinworth Street, London SE11 5AL

British Library Cataloguing in Publication Information Available

Library of Congress Cataloging-in-Publication Data

Names: Mlinar, Courtney, 1957– author.
Title: Embedded and empowered : a practical guide for librarians / Courtney Mlinar.
Description: Lanham : Rowman & Littlefield, [2019] | Series: Practical guides for librarians |
    Includes bibliographical references and index.
Identifiers: LCCN 2018038218 (print) | LCCN 2018053058 (ebook) | ISBN 9781442263611
    (electronic) | ISBN 9781442263604 (pbk. : alk. paper)
Subjects: LCSH: Embedded librarians. | Library personnel management.
Classification: LCC Z682.4.E46 (ebook) | LCC Z682.4.E46 M58 2019 (print) | DDC
    020.92—dc23
LC record available at https://lccn.loc.gov/2018038218

∞™ The paper used in this publication meets the minimum requirements of American
National Standard for Information Sciences—Permanence of Paper for Printed Library
Materials, ANSI/NISO Z39.48-1992.

Printed in the United States of America

Contents

Figures and Tables

◉ Figure

◉ Tables

Preface

What do embedded librarians do, and why do they matter? Embedded librarians build fully engaged partnerships, making a transformative impact both within these embedded communities and library services. The expertise that librarians offer in connecting different groups, information literacy knowledge, and understanding how information is organized and disseminated is invaluable. This proficiency helps to facilitate the sociocultural immersion of a librarian into different organizations. Librarians who are embedded experience recognition for their contributions and enjoy making a difference in the aspirations of the outside group.

Embedded librarianship is not a new concept. Early scholars viewed librarians as fellow researchers. Subject librarians have supported communities with research instruction, collection development, and more over the years. Different levels of support have existed within all types of libraries. This book describes more than supporting communities—the embedded librarian joins and works actively within the outside embedded group as a vital, contributing member.

Embedded librarians from all types of libraries—academic, medical, special, school, and public—find opportunities to form new partnerships and embed their work in a variety of ways. Different levels of embeddedness offer versatility and opportunities for new strategies. Librarians who become teaching partners in academia have transformed the curriculum and integrated into programs of study. Public librarians are part of key community groups, working for social, economic, educational, and cultural non-profit organizations. Medical librarians are members of research teams, residency programs, pharmacy departments, and critical care groups. Librarians recognize the impact of embedded librarianship, making it a hot topic at conferences, but may find little advice on how to start.

Purpose

Librarians are associated with library buildings; that is, a librarian is a person who works in a library. However, a librarian who is empowered with a good understanding of his or her capabilities and library resources can become a strong knowledge partner for organizations beyond the library walls. A practical guide for beginning an embedded librarianship program, designed for librarians who work in all types of libraries, is difficult to find in the professional literature. Most of the recently published literature focuses on embedded librarianship in academia or in health science libraries, with little guidance for librarians who work outside educational systems. Current literature also tends to focus on embedding or integrating the library or its resources, rather than the expert librarian, into academic courses. Journal articles describe mostly individual case studies where librarians are embedded within a specific organization. These works describe what happened but not necessarily how it happened.

There is a gap in the literature for learning the basics for building embedded partnerships. *Embedded and Empowered: A Practical Guide for Librarians* provides workable ideas and shares best practices to embed an organization and create an effective embedded librarian program. This guide helps the librarian work with stakeholders from both the library and the outside organization to create an embedded program from inception to practice. Most librarians are aware of the benefits of embedded librarianship but need help in getting started. An embedded librarian can be established as an essential partner in any working group of people. Information is needed that discusses recommended steps of developing, managing, sustaining, and evaluating an embedded librarianship program that will be applicable to any type of library or librarian. This book focuses on embedding librarians, not libraries, into different organizations. This is a paradigm shift from current literature. An embedded librarian must build a presence that socioculturally embeds the librarian, who is regarded as an expert, into an organization.

Embedded and Empowered: A Practical Guide for Librarians is directed to professional librarians and their managers. Successfully embedded librarians create great relationships between organizations and libraries, easily developing strong library support in user communities. This step-by-step guide includes checklists, reflective exercises, and examples of successful programs. It will help the reader develop an understanding of current trends in embedded librarianship, how librarians are needed, and how to play an essential role within embedded groups such as academic programs, school curriculums, community and political organizations, corporate and law environments, and arts organizations.

Distinctive Features

Embedded and Empowered: A Practical Guide for Librarians offers librarians a formula for success in creating successful embedded programs. Distinctive features include key processes for creating an embedded librarian strategy by analyzing the organizational culture of the outside program, and a set of procedures for moving forward with a workable action plan. Examples from all type of libraries—academic, school, medical, public, and special—describe methods that may be used for embedded programs for planning, implementation, and evaluation. This book also discusses effective communication strategies for promoting the expertise of the embedded librarian and publicizing the impact of the embedded partnership.

Organization

Empowered and Embedded is organized to guide a librarian from any type of library through the course of strategically embedding into an outside organization. It is intended to be read from cover to cover, preparing the librarian to move from theory to action. The content contains proven approaches, providing a systematic design for practical applications, and laying out a clear pathway to a rewarding embedded librarian program.

Chapter 1 introduces embedded librarianship in different types of libraries—academic, school, public, medical. It discusses embedded definitions and describes how libraries have opportunities to be embedded in various types of organizations.

Chapter 2 gives the reader an overview of the evolving practice of embedded librarianship with a brief history and literature review. It discusses how educational support from librarians has progressed to collaborative teaching roles. As a result, embedded librarians find it easier to embed value-added services, no matter the type of library that is providing the services. It emphasizes a different perspective, valuing the importance for examining expertise and the role of the librarian over simply integrating library resources and services within embedded groups.

Chapter 3 introduces practical components for smart planning and goal-setting readiness. It encourages librarians to use an analytical tool, a SWOT analysis, to gain insight to understand the information needs of the outside organization. This type of analysis will help direct decision-making for an impactful venture into embedded librarianship.

Chapter 4 introduces the need to examine the librarian identity within the context of an embedded organization. The same SWOT framework is used as in chapter 3, analyzing librarian professional skill sets, knowledge, and competencies. Exploring and defining expertise, feelings about approaching the embedded program, and learning more about capabilities will help in formulating a vision for creating an embedded strategy.

Chapter 5 calls for reflective thinking for assimilating into the embedded organization. Embedded groups have unique social norms and stakeholder behavior that must be learned so that the librarian has a chance to develop an effective partnership. It is necessary to analyze the personal strengths of the embedded librarian, considering how to work best for building cohesive relationships. This understanding will help smooth communication and productivity issues at the inception of the embedded program.

Chapter 6 gives the embedded librarian a practical method to use in setting goals to create an achievable action plan. It studies the need for manageability and sustainability during the earlier planning stages. The need for setting measurable goals that may be linked to both the embedded group and library is emphasized. Tips for constructing an embedded librarian program with attention to workload and communication are also included in this chapter.

Chapter 7 covers collaborative planning with embedded partners. Creating a plan for initiating, implementing, and managing the embedded librarian program is a part of the initial relationship-building process. This chapter discusses the importance of working together with embedded partners at the onset of goals creation and planning to effectively embed the organization.

Chapter 8 provides methodology for evaluating and making a shared strategic embedded librarian plan. The Stufflebeam program evaluation approach is included to make smart changes as the embedded program is launched. The embedded librarian is encouraged to make informed decisions based on data, partner input, and impact as the plan moves from concept to actualization.

Chapter 9 describes using various technologies to support work outside the library walls. As the embedded librarian program is realized within the outside group, leadership opportunities will arise. This chapter talks about how embedded librarian expertise combined with technology leadership increases the demand for librarian value-added services.

Chapter 10 summarizes this practical guide to embedded librarianship. It discusses how embedded librarians operate as advocates for both library services and librarian expertise. It provides success indicators and encourages embedded librarians to be empowered and engaged in the communities they serve.

Embedded librarians make a difference with partnered organizations, sharing their expertise in information literacy and in understanding how information is organized, classified, and retrieved in all types of publishing models. But what does it mean to call oneself an embedded librarian? The next chapter in embedded librarianship will see continued growth, and a greater demand for embedded library partners from all types of libraries, who may establish thriving embedded librarian programs.

Acknowledgments

Special thanks to my faculty colleagues at Austin Community College, Nova Southeastern University, and Cottey College for their willingness to support and value teaching partnerships for student success. Thanks also to the aspiring librarians with whom I had the honor of teaching and mentoring during their initial forays into embedded librarianship.

Thanks to my patient and talented editor, Sandy Wood, who served as a wise guide throughout the creation of this work. Heartfelt thanks to my family and friends for their loving encouragement during the writing process.

CHAPTER 1

Embedded Librarianship

Defining Moments

IN THIS CHAPTER

▷ Definition of embedded librarianship

▷ Embedded librarian roles in different types of libraries

▷ The hallmarks of a successful embedded librarianship program

▷ Five scenarios illustrating embedded librarian opportunities

---

EMBEDDED LIBRARIANSHIP IS A POPULAR TOPIC within the profession. Over the past ten years, continuing education classes on embedded librarianship have generated high enrollment, and articles are being published frequently in the professional literature from all types of libraries on this subject. Librarians who are actively involved in embedded librarianship enthusiastically recommend this career path to their peers and share motivational stories on how they built their programs. One of the most interesting paradoxes about the timeliness of this topic is that discussions about high engagement and the value of embedded librarians are occurring at the same time that others in the same profession are debating about whether the profession is still relevant in the digital environment.

⦿ Defining the Concept

How Do Librarians Describe the Profession?

Librarians must be able to articulate and describe to others what they do as a profession. How do you describe what you do? Why do librarians matter? The American Library Association began an initiative in 2016 led by its president, Dr. Julie Todaro: "Libraries Transform—The Expert in the Library" (Todaro, 2016), to promote the transformative and engaging work by librarians within the communities they serve (see figure 1.1). Librarians are educators with a unique skill set of understanding information classification and retrieval. Some librarians have difficulty expressing well to others what librarianship is about. When this problem is compounded by public misconceptions of librarianship, the librarian who is interested in partnering and embedding within another organization may self-sabotage his or her own efforts for success. A clearly defined concept of librarianship is a necessary tool for creating good partnerships. It is much easier to become engaged and embedded if a librarian can articulately credential his- or herself. How is librarianship defined? Why do librarians matter?

Figure 1.1. American Library Association "Libraries Transform Campaign" button. This button has a removable panel for writing a short description of the librarian's expertise. For example, the librarian's button could say: "I'm an expert in"—any of these three options: MLA 8th edition, fake news, or digital literacy. *Author, from the reference ALA 2016b*

A useful case study that examines how a public library in Red Hook, New York, transformed its community is available on the ALA Libraries Transform website. The library participated in the Libraries Transforming Communities initiative to learn how libraries may partner within communities. As the library began working with a community group, Red Hook Together, the library director and community leader began to realize they were "willing to be partners with people because [they] wanted to get something out of the partnership. It was transactional" (ALA, 2016a). The library director also realized a shift in her perspective as she worked within the community. "Outreach is when we go out and tell people about all the great stuff we're doing at the library. Engagement is going out and asking people what their dreams are for the community, then identifying what needs to happen in order to achieve those dreams" (ALA, 2016a). Talking to organizations outside the library about what librarians do and why it matters changes dramatically as librarians become more engaged and embedded. That is why it can be daunting to try to explain how librarians can help.

How do you describe what you do? The best script to use is one that includes concepts that raise more questions from your audience. For example, following is a recommended script that may be used in working with a new group or simply as an introduction:

I am a librarian, and I have found that many people are not sure what librarians do nowadays. Here are the important things you need to know:

1. *Not everyone who works in the library is actually a librarian. We employ paraprofessional customer service staff, who assist patrons with checkout, fines, and shelving books or materials, and they are usually situated at the front service desk at any library.*
2. *Librarians have a master's degree in library and/or information science, which means we are experts in discovering how information is organized, classified, and retrieved. Most libraries have at least one professional librarian on staff. College or university libraries usually employ a large number of librarians who teach both face-to-face and online.*
3. *As more information is available online, both free and commercially, librarians find that our profession is even more relevant in the digital environment. Most people have difficulty evaluating information, finding accurate information, and understanding the new publishing formats, e-books, mobile apps, and what will work best for their information needs.*
4. *Librarians vet digital information, subscriptions, and databases and create instructional tools, such as online pathfinders to help point patrons to the best resources for their interests.*

Evaluating information competently is a hot topic that is pointedly referred to in this script. It is an excellent conversation starter for a librarian working in any type of library. The reader will also note that the script emphasizes, boldly, the traditional role of the librarian within this definition. It is critical that librarians realize the value of their role within the context of any organization outside the library.

Defining Librarian Impact

The third and fourth points in the example script discuss the impact librarians may have for library patrons. A solid sense of how librarians can make an impact is also useful in defining embedded librarianship. The expertise and cognitive diversity a librarian offers is a unique and specialized knowledge base that is useful in any embedded environment. Understanding the potential impact of embedded librarianship aids in forming any type of partnership with organizations outside the library. Librarians must be prepared to explain how embedded programs are mutually beneficial as well. Using examples of successful programs may work well to visually define the impact made by embedded librarians. The following textbox gives an example of the impact of embedded librarianship in a middle school library.

EXAMPLE: EMBEDDED MIDDLE SCHOOL LIBRARIAN

The school librarian, whose position has been renamed at least twice since she began working at her school six years ago (technology coordinator, media specialist), is embedded as a teaching partner and curriculum specialist within the sixth-grade faculty. Although the school has a nice physical library space, the *librarian*—the human element—is considered the greatest resource for this group of faculty and students. This librarian has a strong history of collaborating with students, administration, and faculty. She has played a major role in developing a mentoring program within the sixth grade, working with honors students to help slower readers practice and improve their reading. These honors student mentors help struggling students improve their reading skills at the neighboring elementary school as well as the public library. She has forged a strong partnership with the children's librarian at the public library as well as the teen librarian. She team teaches regularly with the middle school faculty and also is a member of the school professional development team. Student reading scores have been rising steadily at both the elementary and middle school as a result of her innovative reading programs.

How Did Embedded Librarianship Begin?

Librarians as educators or teaching partners is not a modern concept. The first issue of the *Library Journal* from October 1876 featured a column written by Samuel Swett Green, the American Library Association's first president, which contained these two core ideas:
   Librarians should:

- Help the reader
- Mingle with the reader

A librarian helping the reader is the major principle behind any reference or Ask a Librarian desk. Most library science or information science degrees require a course in reference, where the librarian is trained in the art of the reference interview and learns about the types of information sources found in a reference collection. There are not many degree programs that offer courses in how to mingle with the reader or experience a minor immersion in the reader's world. Mingling with readers to better understand their daily activities, information needs, and how they seek to fulfill these needs is an important concept within embedded librarianship. The word "mingle" does not convey marketing or selling the library specifically, but more of a socialization process, belonging to another group outside of the library. Much of the professional literature discusses this socialization process in the context of case studies, describing chronologically how individual embedded programs were developed. Librarians initially were embedded in educational programs such as course management systems, as curriculum specialists, subject bibliographers, and later as fellow instructors. Librarians worked outside the library, moving into both physical and virtual classrooms. As technology changed information access and library collections, librarians found their information retrieval skills in high demand. Following are some examples of how changes created by digital information increased the demand for these skills:

- Faculty found it challenging to keep up with emerging technologies, to navigate digital library collections and the internet. Faculty-librarian partnerships called for librarians to apply their expertise and knowledge in classifying, evaluating, and organizing information to address these information challenges.
- Library administration began to realize the need for taking librarians out of the library, physically or virtually, to mingle with readers, to stop waiting for faculty or students to come to the reference desk, or to participate in organizational committee work outside the library walls, thus creating more collaboration and coordination between the librarian and the embedded organization.
- Librarians moved from supporting roles into instructional partnerships with faculty, guest lecturing in classes and creating content for learning.

What Is the Definition of Embedded Librarianship?

The most utilitarian definition for embedded librarianship in higher education appeared in a 2004 article by Barbara Dewey: "Embedding requires more direct and purposeful interaction than acting in parallel with another person, group, or activity. Overt purposefulness makes embedding an appropriate definition of the most comprehensive collaborations for librarians in the higher education community" (Dewey, 2004: 6).

Purposeful collaborations include assigning a librarian to be a liaison for an academic department or a subject librarian for a subject within a department, such as English composition within the humanities department. As student learning outcomes developed that included information literacy concepts, librarians began to assume active roles within these collaborations as teaching partners. Dewey also called for librarians to take a seat at the table in campus-wide initiatives and fund-raising activities as well as facilities and virtual space planning.

In 2003, the United States went to war in Iraq and used embedded journalists as a way to achieve a level of transparency and strategically market the controversial war effort. Journalists were attached to a military unit and were provided protection within the war zone. They trained in boot camp along with U.S. soldiers and assumed a role within their assigned units. Some journalists acquired access to classified information but agreed not to include content in their reporting that would compromise their unit or the war effort. The Dewey article was written in 2004 and drew parallels between librarian and journalist roles within an embedded unit.

The literature describes three important parts of embedded librarianship. The embedded librarian

1. is "an integral part of the whole" (Dene, 2011: 225)
2. is "experiencing, observing the daily life of another group" (Dewey, 2004: 6)
3. "adds value-added services" (Shumaker and Talley, 2009: 21)

This definition takes on more meaning when examined in the context of the culture of the time period when embedded librarianship evolved and the professional literature began to include more articles about this changing role.

Integral Part of the Whole

The embedded librarian becomes an essential element and is accepted as part of the embedded unit within the big picture. This acceptance by higher education faculty was not difficult to accomplish. The academic library traditionally played an important role as a center for teaching and learning. Librarians created pathfinder content, provided bibliographical assistance for faculty and student research, and selected materials to support the curriculum. Subject or liaison librarian appointments created a more personalized pathway to faculty-librarian collaborations that were more faculty and student centered.

As librarians learned more about embedded librarianship, some misconceptions occurred. Successfully embedded librarians recognize the unique skill sets and education possessed by traditional librarianship. Librarians who are not successful as embedded librarians often overstep their knowledge base and attempt to morph into the other group's area. For example, a librarian embedded in a community college history department with a similar educational background as history department faculty needs to maintain the librarian role within the unit. A librarian may be asked to create a rubric to determine if students are selecting the best sources for their research assignment. The rubric may be designed by collaborating with the faculty member and using criteria discussed within the library information literacy instruction taught in class. The librarian may be asked by the faculty member to assign a grade to the students' bibliographies, which is venturing into a faculty instructor role. The librarian should clarify both the faculty and librarian roles at this time. Grades are the responsibility of the faculty, and the instructor is liable in case a student disagrees with a grade, appeals the grade, or pursues a lawsuit. The librarian provides content, presents guest lectures, and may assist with selecting criteria for evaluating sources, but the librarian is usually not named as the instructor for the course. Venturing into these other areas without the instructor designation undermines and dilutes the impact that may be made by a professional librarian. The cognitive diversity a librarian offers to the group as a specialist or consultant outside the subject of the course is the most important contribution to the course and is also the key to becoming an integral part of the whole.

Experiencing, Observing Daily Life

This premise goes hand in hand with Green's statement from 1876 about mingling with the reader. The librarian can take practiced expertise in conducting an effective reference interview to another level by experiencing and observing the daily digital activity and information challenges experienced by the whole group. This idea can be difficult to convey, as the effective librarian needs to maintain the librarian identity while immersing his or her daily life into the group. The expertise brought directly to the group is different from the rest of the group and gives the librarian an opportunity to think reflectively about challenges faced and the goals envisioned by the whole.

Value-Added Services

Every library offers valuable and needed services to its patrons, such as internet access or computer classes. The value-added component in embedded librarianship is the human element. There is a lot of professional literature and formulae readily available that describe the value of libraries. Program planning should think more about what librarians offer, not libraries, in terms of services available. The embedded librarian offers a value-added service, unique to that individual's experience, personality, and energy level. It is the people in the libraries who make an impact. For example, a librarian may be the technology expert within groups, and may find him- or herself thrust into a leadership role as a tech initiative advocate. These accidental leaders may feel unprepared to lead at first, but many librarians find they must lead as they have the needed expertise for partnerships formed within these groups. Librarians understand how information is disseminated, published, purchased, and made available. Even the most experienced researchers benefit from working with a librarian. Colleges with high student retention rates have strong library programs integrated within the curriculum, according to a report prepared by Brown with contributions by Malenfant (ACRL, 2015). A study by Lance, Rodney, and Pennell-Hamilton (2000) illustrated that school districts with professional librarians staffing their libraries see higher student test scores, especially when they work cooperatively with teachers in providing information literacy instruction to both classes and professional development sessions.

Effective Embedded Librarian Roles

Defining concepts of embedded librarianship within the context of different types of libraries requires the librarian to try to draw parallels to make these ideas more meaningful. Many of the examples described in this chapter discuss embedded academic librarians. The following scenarios provide examples of embedded librarianship within an assortment of library types.

Scenario 1: Academic Librarian at a University

Most community college libraries play an active role in information literacy instruction, especially within the humanities curriculum. An embedded librarian in this environment may be involved in departments outside the library in the following roles:

- Attending regular faculty or departmental meetings
- Team teaching as a part of faculty training for new initiatives or courses related to student success or the first-year experience for students
- Creating LibGuides for classes as a customized student portal for a specific research assignment
- Serving on a curriculum or instructional design committee for an academic department
- Creating subject-specific or generic tutorials or instructional videos

Scenario 2: Reference Librarian at a Public Library in a Suburban Community

Trends in public librarians acting as embedded librarians include various governmental partnerships and creating new programs. Roles played by an embedded public librarian include:

- Sustainability partnerships with city government with educational programs, information on the website, or public speaking engagements about recycling
- Partnership with a local pharmacy to engage community members in discussions about vaccinations, dental hygiene, or health information resources

- Facilitating local film festivals, partnering with the high school drama and music programs
- Working shoulder to shoulder with the local Red Cross using technology in a triage setting during a natural disaster to help citizens apply for federal aid programs

Scenario 3: High School Librarian in a Small Town

Smaller-town school librarians often find innovative ways to form collaborations not only within their own school district, but also with community non-profits and public libraries.

- Partnering with the high school counselors for the annual college fair event, providing information resources, and moderating classes that inform parents about paying for college, educational alternatives to college, or how to evaluate a college
- Team teaching with the chemistry and biology departments at the high school about how to find scientific information, and how to read a scientific article and understanding scientific terminology
- Collaborating with the public library for a community-wide One Read program, creating shared LibGuides, or integrating the parent-teacher-student organization with Friends of the Library for related events
- Facilitating the foreign language department meeting with local English as a second language mentors

Scenario 4: School Librarian at an Elementary School in a Large City

School librarians are often solo librarians, even at large elementary schools in an urban environment. Embedded librarians are not required to leave the library in order to be effective. Examples of embedded librarians operating as solo elementary school librarians include:

- Creating a LibGuide of open educational resources for faculty and presenting the use of them at faculty meetings
- Facilitating shared programmatic, cross-disciplinary educational experiences with the library as the hub or learning space for these programs
- Writing a monthly newsletter or weekly blog on suggested resources available online to supplement class materials
- Providing professional development day content, leading sessions on educational technology or open resources

Scenario 5: Hospital Librarian at a Rural Hospital

Hospital librarians are also solo librarians, who may have additional responsibilities for continuing education program coordination. An embedded hospital librarian may assume roles such as:

- Coordinating with clinical faculty to provide health literacy instruction to residents
- Facilitating discussions between departments such as nursing and pharmacy to discuss using mobile devices and apps in regular care practice
- Partnering with the physical therapy department to create a makerspace

- Providing resources for copyright compliance and citation assistance for publishing doctors
- Establishing a consumer health question-and-answer relationship within the hospital community

⊚ Hallmarks for Successful Programs

Successful embedded librarian programs exemplify best practices in information literacy, collaborative partnerships, and very busy libraries. Libraries often see their circulation desk statistics increase dramatically as a result of embedded programs. Partnerships between librarians and patron groups produce a new awareness of library services and resources, which these new patrons are enthusiastic about using. The library's administration has the power to make or break an embedded librarian program. Embedded librarians must work closely with their administrative staff and supervisors to create a plan of action that is aligned with the library's mission and goals. Communication with funding partners and important stakeholders is an important priority for both the librarian and the administration. Increased communication also adds a layer of visibility that may positively affect library funding and community support.

Pervasive Information Literacy Goals

Librarians see themselves as the process owners for developing information literacy programs and setting literacy goals within the communities they serve. This perspective is strongly supported by the work of the library profession in setting standards for information literacy, identifying important skills, and creating multiple instructional tools for teaching this subject. These efforts can be multiplied exponentially if librarians share the responsibility for a community's information literacy goals. A shared definition and vision for information literacy within a library's community is a very powerful hallmark observed in effective embedded librarian programs. Giving away this ownership produces a multi-disciplinary user group that is educated and prepared to wade intelligently and critically through the daily and pervasive information environment together. Sharing the process rather than acting as process owners also leads to more questions about information, increasing librarian activity and interaction within the group. It is an interesting contradiction: the more competent the group members become in evaluating information, the more they want to learn and the more they seek to utilize and engage the skills and competency of the embedded librarian.

Communication and Strategic Planning

Support for any embedded librarian program from administration is the catalyst that leads to success. Any change in traditional reference librarian roles must be communicated and managed well by library administration. The change should be a part of strategic and budget planning, and the rest of the staff should be informed and involved. A successful plan leads to a marked increase in library usage, and additional staff or librarians may be required for support. The head administrator for the library may also want to contact and discuss entry points into the embedded unit with the respective administrator of that unit. For example, a library director for a health sciences library may assign a librarian to create a liaison-type role within the nursing department, leading to a deeper embedded role with shared funding. The director may want to discuss these plans with the head of the nursing department, assist with introductions, and arrange for the librarian to attend departmental or related committees, such as curriculum or textbook committees. Nursing faculty will easily support a librarian assuming a role within their department that has been articulated and defined by the nursing department administration.

The librarian may set up library orientation meetings with new faculty and discover widespread support from existing faculty who understand this librarian will be working together with the rest of the department. Planning together will help provide reference desk coverage while the librarian is working outside the library as well. If the health sciences library has a large staff of librarians who are embedded in different programs, coordination and teamwork will be needed to provide assistance at the library while these embedded librarians are working within their assigned departments. If the library has a smaller-sized staff, more creative solutions may be needed, such as virtual reference help or the use of chat software. Librarians also may choose to meet with faculty or students by appointment, until additional reference support can be funded or additional positions filled.

Library Visibility and Stakeholders

The visibility of the library, within academia, public communities, hospitals, schools, and corporate organizations, affects funding, local support, usage, facilities, and services. Librarians, library administration, and stakeholders who are advocates for libraries must aim to increase visibility in order to thrive. No matter how beautiful the physical space or how prominently located, visibility rests squarely on the shoulders of the library's professional librarian staff. The more librarians mingle with and serve their communities, the easier it is for stakeholders to understand the impact of the librarians and why they matter within these communities.

Embedded librarianship takes these talented individuals out of the library to work. A priority for work that is visible and makes an impact within embedded communities garners stakeholder support as well as support of the embedded unit. Successful embedded librarian programs call attention to the ways libraries support their communities and attract more people to the library as well as the library's online resources. It's a win-win situation for both the library and the community, and library stakeholders and administrators who recognize and support these embedded librarians are strong indicators for successful programs.

ⓖ Key Points

This chapter has examined how embedded librarianship is defined as well as the various concepts associated with this role. Selected scenarios were included that illustrate these concepts.

- Roles of embedded librarians include:
  - Comprehensive integration into other groups
  - Cultural immersion and collaboration within these groups, observing and participating in the daily lives of these groups
  - Contributing knowledge about organizing, classifying, retrieving information
  - Providing valuable services unique to the librarian profession

- Supporting and/or partnering with others outside the library to realize shared goals
- Scenarios for embedded librarians include academic librarians, public librarians, school librarians, and hospital librarians.
- Examples for the types of embedded librarian roles within different types of libraries illustrate these roles in different contexts.
- Hallmarks for successful programs include strong administrative support—from library administration and stakeholders and administration for the embedded units.

The next chapter will outline an in-depth literature review of programs, which may inspire the reader to look at embedded librarianship in new ways.

References

ACRL (Association of College and Research Libraries). 2015. *Academic Library Contributions to Student Success: Documented Practices from the Field.* Prepared by Karen Brown. Contributions by Kara J. Malenfant. Chicago: Association of College and Research Libraries, 2015. http://www.ala.org/acrl/sites/ala.org.acrl/files/content/issues/value/contributions_report.pdf.

ALA (American Library Association). 2016a. "Case Study: Red Hook (N.Y.) Public Library: One Small Win Creates Huge Ripples of Change." http://www.ala.org/transforminglibraries/libraries-transforming-communities/case-studies/redhook.

ALA (American Library Association). 2016b. "Libraries Transform Campaign. Libraries Transform." http://www.ala.org/transforminglibraries/libraries-transform-campaign.

Dene, Jezmynne. 2011. "Embedded Librarianship at the Claremont Colleges." In *Embedded Librarians: Moving beyond One-Shot Instruction*, edited by Cassandra Kvenild and Kaijsa Calkins, 219–28. Chicago: American Library Association.

Dewey, Barbara I. 2004. "The Embedded Librarian: Strategic Campus Collaborations." *Resource & Sharing Information Networks* 17, no. 1–2: 5–17.

Green, Samuel Swett. 1876. "Personal Relations between Librarians and Readers." *Library Journal* 1, no. 1 (October): 74–81.

Lance, Keith Curry, Marcia J. Rodney, and Christine Pennell-Hamilton. 2000. *Measuring Up to Standards: The Impact of School Library Programs and Information Literacy in Pennsylvania Schools.* Greensburg, PA: Pennsylvania Citizens for Better Libraries.

Shumaker, David, and Mary Talley. 2009. *Models of Embedded Librarianship: Final Report.* Special Libraries Association. http://hq.sla.org/pdfs/embeddedlibrarianshipfinalrptrev.pdf.

Todaro, Julie B. 2016. "The Expert in the Library." *American Libraries*, July 20, 2016. https://americanlibrariesmagazine.org/2016/07/20/libraries-transform-expert-library/.

Further Reading

Becnel, Kim, Robin A. Moeller, and Jon C. Pope. 2016. "Powerful Partnerships: The Worth of Embedding Masters Level Library Science Students in Undergraduate Classes." *Journal of Education for Library and Information Science* 57, no. 1: 31–42. https://eric.ed.gov/?q=embedded+librarian&ft=on&id=EJ1090746.

Blanchard, Ken, Jane Ripley, and Eunice Parisi-Carew. 2015. *Collaboration Begins with You: Be a Silo Buster.* Oakland, CA: Berrett-Koehler.

Cooper, I. Diane, and Janet A. Crum. 2013. "New Activities and Changing Roles of Health Sciences Librarians: A Systematic Review, 1990–2012." *Journal of Medical Library Association* 101, no. 4 (October): 268–77. https://doi.org/10.3163/1536-5050.101.4.008.

CHAPTER 2

Embedded Librarianship as An Evolving Practice

TRACING THE HISTORY of embedded librarianship is complicated—different words and job titles are used in an attempt to capture descriptions of new or changing roles and an evolving practice. Chapter 1 discussed hallmarks and definitions for embedded librarians but did not delve into closely related librarian roles or different levels of engagement within the embedded target organization. One of the most interesting observations one may find in performing a literature search for embedded librarianship is that a new advocacy begins to arise for librarian expertise.

History and Literature Review of Embedded Librarianship

Literature for embedded librarianship traces emerging roles of librarians who have embraced transformational change and relationship building within their communities. The advancement of new technologies has affected librarian roles and responsibilities as well as how communities interact with library workers. In 2006, an ACRL Roundtable on Technology and Change in Academic Libraries concluded that the roles of librarians and libraries needed to change and respond to shifting needs of faculty and students in research and education. Librarians were advised to act to reconfigure roles and "move beyond parameters of earlier times to pursue new modes of serving their institutions" (ACRL Roundtable on Technology and Change in Academic Libraries, 2006). This reconfiguration proved challenging because transformational change management can be difficult and messy.

According to Anderson and Anderson (2010), in an article about the different facets of change, developmental change "improves what you are currently doing rather than creates something new. Improving existing skills, processes, methods, performance standards, or conditions can all be developmental changes." Adding a new library service, such as laptop checkout, is an example of developmental change in libraries. In this example staff must develop and learn new processes and possibly acquire new technology skills for troubleshooting laptop or connectivity issues. Timelines for projects of this type are set, and goal attainment is measurable. Another type of change, transitional change, "replaces 'what is' with something completely new" (Anderson and Anderson, 2010). Examples may include replacing an integrated library system (ILS) used for more than ten years at the library with a new ILS, such as a change from Ex Libris to SirsiDynix. The library staff must learn new terminology and how to use the software, but the change does not require an organizational shift or change in job responsibilities. These innovations are managed in ways similar to developmental change, and results may be detailed in easily identified measurable outcomes.

Transformational change affects the workplace in a different way, often creating new roles and processes that operate in newer environments or workplace cultures. Embedded librarianship is a transformational change in the integration of librarians and their work within communities. It emerged as a major trend in academic librarianship that may be traced in professional literature from the 1990s to the 2000s. As college and university librarian responsibilities included more teaching expectations plus a growing number of information literacy instruction requests, librarians found new ways to partner with faculty. Academic library spaces were being transformed into learning commons areas, and added digital resource options began to dominate library collections. Library spaces looked different, and librarians began to perform more work outside the library walls.

According to a review of learning spaces in academic libraries by Turner, Welch, and Reynolds, technology influenced the way "people exchanged and accessed information . . . many believed that digital information . . . would gradually replace books" (2013: 227). The development of the information commons spaces offered new ways to offer "'teaching moments' for library staff" (2013: 228). An ethnographic study by Haglund and Olsson from 2005 to 2006 found that patrons were using Google for research, indicating they did not realize there was a need for library instruction or resources in research, plus the library was changing from being primarily the place for researchers to find research help to an area for social learning for undergraduate students (2008). Many libraries were also reconfiguring spaces to create more student group study areas. Increased communication to faculty was needed as these changes occurred. The Haglund and Olsson study showed "researchers having less and less understanding of what difference librarian competencies can make" (2008: 56). These changes in information-seeking behaviors questioned the competencies of librarians within research institutions, and as a result, librarian job descriptions and identities were transformed, revised, and reworked.

Librarianship job postings also experienced rapid job description changes with new technology and teaching competencies. A study on a new emerging technology library position by Radniecki in 2013 included a literature review about hiring trends. This article describes how "libraries strive to leverage new technologies to update service models in reference, instruction, and access service departments to meet their patrons' point-of-need preferences in location, device choice, and information seeking behaviors." Radniecki collected job posting data from the American Library Association JobLIST database from 2007 to 2013 and examined job description trends. In addition to anticipated job responsibilities in emerging technology areas, new job duty trends in the areas of collaboration, liaison tasks, and trendspotting were noted in this article.

Job titles for librarians have changed, and these name and identity changes create a mixed variety of results in searching the literature for journal articles using the keyword term "embedded librarians." Terminology in journal articles and books used interchangeably to describe embedded librarians include blended librarian, liaison librarian, informationist, subject librarian, branch librarian, clinical librarian, and embedded librarian. Diane Cooper and Janet Crum wrote a systematic review in 2013 that describes the changing roles of health science librarians—a subset within academic librarianship. Job titles found within this group alone included

> embedded librarians (such as clinical informationist, bioinformationist, public health informationist, disaster information specialist); systematic review librarian; emerging technologies librarian; continuing medical education librarian; grants development librarian; and data management librarian. New roles identified through job announcements were digital librarian, metadata librarian, scholarly communication librarian, and translational research librarian. (Cooper and Crum, 2013: 268)

These new roles "reinforce the librarian's role as a specialized professional participating in new technology to distribute information (knowledge) to their clients and to participate in expanded roles outside the library" (Cooper and Crum, 2013: 275).

The experimentation with using new job titles to reflect new librarian roles makes it challenging to trace a clear pathway to embedded librarianship within the literature. For this reason, a methodology was used to organize and discuss the literature in terms of the depth of the embedded partnerships formed as well as the sustainability of these programs. This chapter's discussion will focus on three specifically defined roles (see table 2.1) in the context of a rubric to compare degrees or dimensions of embeddedness. Levels or degrees of embedded librarianship are:

- Level 1: blended librarian
- Level 2: liaison librarian
- Level 3: embedded librarian

This chapter will also describe the key articles that help define these roles that contribute to this multi-dimensional picture of embedded librarianship in the context of establishing different degrees or levels of embeddedness.

Table 2.1. Defined Roles of the Three Levels or Degrees of Embedded Librarians

	BLENDED LIBRARIAN	SUBJECT OR LIAISON LIBRARIAN	EMBEDDED LIBRARIAN
Definitions Used in This Chapter	Refers to a librarian with a blended skill or knowledge set, such as "an academic librarian who combines the traditional skill set of librarianship with the information technologist's hardware/software skills, and the instructional or educational designer's ability to apply technology appropriately in the teaching-learning process" (Bell and Shank, 2004).	Librarian whose position requires him or her to provide support services to a group outside the library walls—a subject bibliographer, a business librarian, a music librarian. Some embedded services may be provided (Drewes and Hoffman, 2010).	Librarian who not only develops a partnership with a group outside the library walls, but also becomes an active contributor to the responsibilities of that group.

Multi-dimensional Roles Related to Embedded Librarians

Level 1: Blended Librarians

Steven Bell and John Shank have written extensively about academic librarians establishing the blended librarian role since 2004. As library content and collections as well as academic course management ventured into digital technologies, librarians applied their knowledge and skills toward multiple technological challenges. Bell and Shank call this shifting role "blended librarianship" (2004: 372). Librarians originally assumed a supporting role, helping information technology (IT) workers understand what technology faculty and students needed for learning, but quickly it evolved into an important partnership. Librarians partnered with IT department workers to host digital collections—e-books, streaming media—and found value in these relationships. Academic librarians, IT specialists, and faculty worked together to learn how to train patrons to use library resources in these new digital environments. Users consulted librarians at public and academic libraries for assistance in purchasing and using new digital information formats, software, and hardware. Librarians collaborated with both IT staff and faculty and made valuable connections across the academic disciplines. Librarians and IT staff shared a concern for privacy and information security, and also shared a concern for accessibility to information with faculty and students. Bell and Shank write "that the future of academic librarianship depends on our collective ability to integrate [library] services and practices into the teaching and learning process" (2004: 373). They developed six principles of blended librarianship:

1. "Taking leadership positions as campus innovators and change agents . . ."
2. "Committing to developing campus-wide information literacy initiatives . . ."
3. "Designing instructional and educational programs and classes to assist patrons in using library services and learning information literacy . . ."
4. "Collaborating and engaging in dialogue with instructional technologies and designers . . ."
5. "Implementing adaptive, creative, proactive, and innovative change in library instruction . . ."
6. "Transforming our relationship with faculty requires that we concentrate our efforts to assist them in integrating technology and library resources into (hybrid/

blended) courses. We must also add to our traditional role a new capacity for collaboration to improve student learning and outcome assessment in the areas of information access, retrieval, and integration."

(Bell and Shank, 2004: 374)

These recommendations for new roles recognized the need to "raise awareness, promote the contributions librarians can make, and create change . . . [that] lays the groundwork for deeper integration of our profession into the mainstream functions of higher education" (Bell and Shank, 2004: 374, 375).

As blended librarians led campus technology initiatives, they grappled with changing library collection formats, new electronic resources, vendors, and a push for competency in website design and usability. Online learning management systems were used in distance learning as well as in hybrid classrooms. Faculty sought assistance from librarians for instructional design, and librarians worked to create a virtual presence within courses to help students connect to the brick-and-mortar library. These blended librarians worked closely with faculty and students to address learning outcomes related to information literacy and computer competence. As the size of digital library collection grew, library instruction programs transformed librarians' roles with faculty and students. Librarians and faculty created important partnerships with collaborative work on educational technology and library resource integration within courseware. Faculty and librarians experimented with adaptive, innovative educational technology. Social learning strengthened these relationships, and librarians gained seats at the technology tables within their institutions, serving in campus-wide technology committees. Mingling technology skills with librarianship greatly increased the visibility of librarians within academia.

Bell and Shank later encouraged [blended] librarians to create new roles as campus change agents at higher education institutions as a "blueprint for redefining the teaching and learning role of academic librarians" (2004: 372). Software programs for librarians were developed to aid in creating online information literacy tutorials and pathfinders, such as the Springshare LibGuides. Now that the library collection was available even when the doors were closed, librarians found ways to help users by creating LibGuides for both library online tutorials and learning objects. Multiple access points including mobile library apps were developed to guide students and faculty to the most relevant information. Library science degree programs offered courses in online information retrieval systems and web design. These changes in technology did not create blended librarians, but rather librarians saw opportunities through instructional technology to create new partnerships and relationships with their users. According to a 2013 blog entry by Amanda Hovious, there was an "increasing number of instructional design librarian jobs" Hovious also points out that

> having a knowledge foundation in instructional design methods (ADDIE), instructional theories, and educational psychology is vitally important . . . [and] the future of academic libraries (and even public libraries to some extent) will be dependent upon the recognition of this skill set as an important key to the transformation of libraries into true learning spaces. (Hovious, 2013)

As Bell later states, the blended librarian "concept was an early attempt at acknowledging the value of integrating instructional design into the existing librarian skill set" (2016).

Distance learning online and competency-based learning was an influential trend that paralleled these rapid technological changes in education. Delivering education online required the institution to provide evidence that learning was taking place and students were mastering the online content. A culture of evidence or assessment that marked student competencies developed. The Association of College and Research Libraries (ACRL) *Information Literacy Standards* (see textbox), rescinded in 2016, were a response to these changes and created a basis to assess IL skills and demonstrate competencies. These *IL Standards* helped create a basis for a competency-based curriculum for instruction librarians' use. These standards, used extensively throughout academia for rubrics in assessing student learning in the area of information literacy, have been replaced by the *Framework for Information Literacy for Higher Education*, which was published and filed in 2015, and officially adopted in 2016 (see textbox). In 2011, ACRL adopted new *Standards for Libraries in Higher Education*, "positioning libraries as leaders in assessment and continuous improvement on their campuses . . . and providing a comprehensive framework using an outcomes-based approach." Student learning outcomes and their measurement implemented more accountability, established benchmarks for learning, and documented librarians' "contributions to institutional effectiveness" (ACRL, 2011).

ACRL *INFORMATION LITERACY STANDARDS*

"Information literacy forms the basis for lifelong learning. It is common to all disciplines, to all learning environments, and to all levels of education. It enables learners to master content and extend their investigations, become more self-directed, and assume greater control over their own learning. An information literate individual is able to:

- Determine the extent of information needed
- Access the needed information effectively and efficiently
- Evaluate information and its sources critically
- Incorporate selected information into one's knowledge base
- Use information effectively to accomplish a specific purpose
- Understand the economic, legal, and social issues surrounding the use of information, and access and use information ethically and legally"

(ACRL, 2000)

FRAMEWORK FOR INFORMATION LITERACY FOR HIGHER EDUCATION

- Authority Is Constructed and Contextual
- Information Creation as a Process
- Information Has Value
- Research as Inquiry
- Scholarship as Conversation
- Searching as Strategic Exploration

(ACRL, 2015)

BLENDED LIBRARIAN JOB POSTING

Job title: Emerging technology librarian at ABC College

Job duties specific to blended librarianship: Collaboration with IT department to maintain library presence in Blackboard, develops digital initiatives (tablet/ laptop loan program), programming for makerspaces, instructional design for library tutorials.

Academic libraries were not the only type affected by new competency expectations. Similarly written student information literacy competencies also appeared in the health professions and other degree programs with research components. Student learning outcomes and their assessment were used in both online educational delivery and face-to-face classrooms. Libraries in colleges and universities began to develop integrated instruction programs with degree programs to address specific information literacy outcomes. Once librarians assumed a sense of ownership in the area of information literacy, faculty and librarians created team-teaching and curriculum partnerships. As pedagogical relationships developed between librarians and academic departments, library administration at many colleges and universities assigned new liaison roles to these librarians. These new roles helped create more stable partnerships and expectations for responsibility for IL student learning outcomes.

Level 2: Liaison Librarians

There are many different names for liaison librarians: subject librarian, subject specialist, library liaison, academic department librarian (e.g., business librarian, sciences librarian, music librarian), and subject bibliographer, to name a few. The concepts behind the names include the librarian who is assigned to a specific group—a type of personalized, relationship-forming model for either collection development and/or instructional services. Church-Duran published an article in 2017 that traced the development of liaison librarianship. Her brief description notes that liaison librarians work on collection development, but also "reference or research consultation, integration of library instruction into the curriculum, and scholarly communication education. . . . This desire to better connect with users marked an early inroad into an engagement-based approach to librarianship" (259). Librarian services could be customized according to liaison departmental needs. An evaluation of the University of Florida Health Sciences liaison program in 2006 queried faculty and found communication, workload, and library resources usage had increased with the departments with librarian liaisons. Positive faculty responses included the following:

- "I think it is a very valuable resource that increases faculty productivity."
- "We have an ongoing active professional relationship. Our degree program is greatly enhanced by this."
- "My research and teaching productivity and efficacy have increased."

(Tennant et al., 2006)

The University of Minnesota Librarian Position Framework shared by Williams in her 2009 ARL report identified important categories of liaison responsibilities—the "holy trinity" (Williams, 2009)—of reference, instruction, and collection development (Church-Duran, 2017). The liaison staffing model was designed to assist faculty in teaching, learning, academic curriculum consultations, research, and, especially in health sciences, provide support materials for accreditation visits. A follow-up report by Jaguszewski and Williams in 2013 identified roles for liaisons beyond the earlier described "holy trinity," including "research services, digital scholarship, user experience, copyright and scholarly communication." This report also advised librarians to advocate for libraries, serving as "ambassadors of change."

Liaison librarian partners worked actively on departmental curriculum committees, team taught with departmental faculty/guest lectured in research assignments within the department's course offerings, and worked on curricular design with faculty. Specific liaison librarians were branded as the primary contact between the library and the liaison department, a "personal librarian" approach (Kolowich, 2010). Since large collections of library resources were available online, both students and faculty were not coming into the library to research. The liaison librarian role designated a point of contact for on-line users for assistance on projects, papers, and help. This role also ensured that library resources were aligned with the academic department, providing academic support and increasing awareness of library services.

LIAISON LIBRARIAN JOB POSTING

Job title: Business librarian at XYZ University

Liaison duties: Attends business department meetings, creates LibGuides as subject guides for various business majors (finance, real estate, accounting, etc.), handles acquisitions and purchase requests for the department, weeds the print business collections, selects business databases and print journal collection, teaches information literacy classes as requested by business faculty.

Not all colleges and universities adopted the liaison staffing model, preferring a subject generalist approach that created IL content and learning objects that were more generic and modular in nature. These librarians also actively worked with faculty, especially in providing library instruction for research assignments. The generalist staffing model worked well, and librarians were often invited to have an online component within the learning management system. Librarians created more subject-specific content within these online courses and also linked students to the more generic IL tutorials and learning tools such as LibGuides or "how to use the library" tutorials.

Level 3: Embedded Librarians

The embedded librarian model evolved from both blended and liaison librarianship. In the new *Roles and Strengths for Teaching Librarians* document adopted by the ARCL Board of Directors in 2017, a revision of the ACRL *Standards for Proficiencies for Instruction Librarians and Coordinators* (ACRL, 2007), recommendations for practice include a teaching partner role, as noted in the textbox.

ACRL *ROLES AND STRENGTHS FOR TEACHING LIBRARIANS*

- Advocate
- Coordinator
- Instructional Designer
- Lifelong Learner
- Leader
- Teacher
- Teaching Partner

(ACRL, 2017)

The partnership element differentiates the embedded librarian from the earlier described dimensions. The librarian responsibilities transform from a supporting role to an educational/informational partner. The relationship between the librarian and the embedded group is changed to an integrated model where the librarian is viewed as a valued part of the embedded group. This role evolved as the skill sets and cognitive diversity of blended and/or liaison librarians began to offer value-added contributions to departments outside library spaces. Librarians began to develop and team teach a sequential series of active learning sessions to address different fail points in research-related assignments (Sullivan and Porter, 2016). The ACRL *Roles and Strengths* document describes the librarian bringing an "information literacy perspective and expertise to the partnership" (2017). Embedded librarians work to create sustainable partnerships with outside departments that work together for a shared educational mission.

EMBEDDED LIBRARIAN JOB POSTING

Job title: Nursing informationist

Job duties: Regular guest lecturer in all courses with research assignments, provides clinical rounds support, works with nursing department on embedding information literacy components throughout the curriculum, serves on both library and nursing department committees.

There are several common misconceptions about embedded librarianship and how it works. One of the most common misconceptions is related to the roles assumed within academic teaching partnerships. Academic librarians with faculty relationships are often invited to guest lecture, collaborate on course content, and partner in instructional design. Guest lecturers are invited to lecture in a particular subject area due to advanced expertise in that subject. Student grading is the primary responsibility of the instructor, and the librarian teaching partner, if not named as an instructor for the course, should not grade the students. If the librarian is the instructor for the course, such as a one-credit course on information literacy, then the librarian assumes full responsibility for assessing student learning outcomes and producing a final grade for each student within the course. A teaching partner or guest lecturer has different responsibilities for student learning and may help develop an assignment, quiz, or rubric to assess this learning but should not discuss grades with students or assume responsibility for determining the final grade for the course. This guest lecturer–type role with lesser responsibility allows the librarian the time to be embedded within multiple courses at the same time as a resource personalized to the students within the class.

Another common misconception about embedded librarians involves the idea of selling the library and, along those same lines, that only extroverted or sales-type personalities are successful in this role. Most librarians, when asked a reference question, will respond with library resources as well as freely available sources to help fulfill the information need. Is this selling the library? Perhaps it could be viewed in that way, but most library collections are created and maintained so as to directly address anticipated users' information needs. Librarians often guide users to their collections to help answer reference questions. To that end, librarians often make presentations to their communities to increase awareness of new or important resources, essentially marketing or promoting library resources that have already been purchased by the users' tuition, fees, taxes, or community resources.

Table 2.2. Levels of Embedded Librarians

	BLENDED LIBRARIAN	LIAISON LIBRARIAN	EMBEDDED LIBRARIAN
Responsibilities for Projects	Reactive: Librarian responds to requests by various outside groups or individuals on an individual basis. Example: teaches classes on using technology, such classes on citation software in higher education or how to use Word to write a resumé at a public library.	Assigned: Librarian is assigned to a specific group and responds to single transactions and requests within the outside department as requested, may establish integrated projects on an annual basis.	Proactive: Librarian is authorized by both the library and the outside group to participate as an embedded librarian (Andrews, 2015) in multiple ongoing projects and roles within the outside group, such as a key committee member, frequent guest lecturer, curriculum development, strategic planning, and continuing education for outside organization.
Partnership	Responsive service model—librarian responds to requests.	Responsive, customized, knowledge management services (Vassilakaki and Moniarou-Papaconstantinou, 2015)—the librarian provides services both responsively to outside group needs and routinely to group expectations.	Sustainable and strategic partnership—librarian collaborates and partners with the group to create and develop mutual projects related to the educational process or success of the outside team.
Teaching	Supplemental IL classes, LibGuides, or tutorials are developed as requested or may result from multiple questions at the public service desk.	Integrated one-shot classroom instruction is common but not required for all core classes in the liaison department.	Information literacy instruction and reference help are embedded within core classes and faculty development. The librarian and faculty work together to evaluate and improve student learning outcomes and develop the course curriculum.

Although library resources are commonly used and promoted by embedded librarians, the personality type of the librarian does not have to be extroverted. Embedded partnerships are relationships formed by mutual interests in learning, literacy, and credible information. These relationships, like any other, are formed by multiple personality types. Librarians may find themselves in very interesting partnerships where their role as a librarian is valued and the connections they make are influential to those outside their profession. Table 2.2 shows comparisons for the three levels of embedded responsibilities.

Although the largest amount of the literature on embedded librarianship discusses new roles assumed by academic librarians, it is important to also examine these same roles as they may apply in a different context—for different types of libraries.

Paradigm Shift: Librarians, Not Libraries

Literature that details different roles assumed by embedded librarians describes a paradigm shift: an emphasis on the value of the work of librarians, within and outside their libraries. Much has been written to brand and market libraries and to describe the importance of libraries within the communities they serve. Advocacy for librarians is a major paradigm shift that focuses on the talent and contributions of a profession that is largely misunderstood by the general public. Librarianship is a people-centered profession, which creates content, curates resources for their user communities, and develops new services. Following are examples of what embedded librarianship looks like in different types of libraries.

Embedded Academic Librarians

A 2016 article by Sullivan and Porter describe "embedded team teaching" as the "gold standard" for their institution. "The ideal to strive for is a situation in which librarians and teaching faculty are complete equals working together on the content and coverage of the information literacy components of the course" (2016: 34). The goal of embedding a librarian fully within every information literacy aspect as described may be hard to attain, especially due to a lack of time for both faculty and the librarian. This article emphasizes that "when libraries and information literacy are authentically integrated into a course, students realize that it is not a separate module or something that does not require their complete attention. It demonstrates that the subject faculty member values these components and sees them as integral to the course, which students are keenly sensitive to" (2016: 37). Students follow the faculty example in viewing the librarian expertise as value added to learning the subject matter.

Embedded Public Librarians

Cheryl Becker argues in her 2012 blog entry that embedded librarianship is "most needed in public libraries" because "embedded librarianship positions libraries in the center of their communities. . . . Librarians have the power to change lives and build community—but to do this, we have to leave our desks, leave our buildings, and show the community what a powerful tool we are." Barbara Alvarez, author of *Embedded Business Librarianship for the Public Librarian* (2016), wrote an article for *Public Libraries Online* in 2014 that describes the difference an embedded public librarian can make for local businesses. Alvarez recommends librarian involvement in non-profit business associations such as the local chamber of commerce and attendance at other organizations where business owners find continuing education and professional development opportunities. She encourages librarians to leave the library in order to serve the business community with library services and online resources. "Embedded librarianship is important to the business community and while they may not often consider the library as a resource, they are a group that can really benefit from the library's services. Job seekers and small business owners don't have limitless time or money; they need valuable information and assistance on a limited budget" (Alvarez, 2014). The embedded librarian may seek partners within the business community and bring the library to the local businesses instead of expecting them to come into the library for assistance and information.

Embedded Health Sciences Librarians

Embedded librarians who partner with various health professions make up another large part of the professional literature on this topic. Health librarianship does not require an additional degree, and most librarians learn how to help answer questions by skillfully conducting a great reference interview. As librarians work closely and develop teaching partnerships at various institutions, these librarians often discover their knowledge of how information is evaluated and how health literacy is developed to be an important skill within the context of the surrounding professions. For example, Raimondo and colleagues (2014) outlined how the librarians at the University of Maryland (UM) began to provide health literacy training and a health consent form review service for principal investigators involved in research using human subjects. The librarians offered training on communicating with patients and included information on patients' levels of understanding consent forms as research subjects, readability, and understanding the patient's perspective. Their work led to greater human subject participation in research studies, increased library visibility, and stronger faculty and administrative relationships. The librarians were embedded into the research teams—at first to aid with health literacy, and, as the research team became familiar with the UM librarians' expertise, they developed strong partnerships and embedded librarian relationships.

Hospital librarians, often solo librarians, have made contributions, such as adding to the content included in electronic health records, by becoming embedded in major committees outside the library walls. An article by Exempla Healthcare hospital librarians Brandes, Wells, and Bandy describes their collaboration with the chief medical information officer in integrating important "point-of-care resources into the EMR, providing evidence for computerized provider order entry (CPOE) sets and collaborating with members of Exempla's Evidence-Based Advisory Committee (EBAC)" (2013: 359). This collaboration resulted in a change in protocol in this health care system, expanding embedded librarian roles in hospital advisory committees for improved evidence-based care.

A similar embedded librarian role occurred during the same year at the LSU Health Sciences Library and LSU Health Shreveport Clinics. Tarver and colleagues (2013) describe a collaboration to connect clinical patients to reliable consumer health information by linking personal health electronic records to MedlinePlus, the consumer health resource from the National Library of Medicine. This article discusses the problems embedded librarians may encounter in these types of collaborations, such as patient care questions out of the scope of the librarian's areas of expertise. Librarians quickly learned how to redirect these types of questions to more appropriate recipients.

Evidence-based practice has been a hot topic within both health sciences librarianship and continuing education for the health professions. Although hospital librarians are often tasked with organizing continuing education (CE) for medical professionals, librarians worked to embed information literacy into this type of curriculum, similar to how academic librarians were embedded into courses. Black and Ballance (2013) describe how they developed a CE course for nurses at the Georgia Health University medical center as well as for medical librarians in the area to learn about evidence-based theory and practice. The embedded librarians worked to approve this course for both MLA CE credit and Georgia Nursing Association contact hours. Evidence-based nursing practices and hospital librarian partnerships have created mutually beneficial relationships that have raised the standards of patient care. Another benefit found in forming these relationships with librarians has contributed to nurses earning more advanced degrees. Educational standards for nursing have changed, and hospital librarians have played important roles in integrating research skills into continuing education classes to support research conducted by nurses in pursuit of a higher degree.

Another embedded librarian trend involves not only active partnering but the leading new initiatives in medical clinics and hospitals. Most of the examples listed earlier in the chapter discuss how a librarian may become embedded into an existing or newly formed group; however, the librarian may also be the creator of the embedded group. Medical librarians at various academic medical centers, hospitals, and universities have helped lead campus initiatives in mobile app collection development and selection. iPad initiatives led by librarians at Nova Southeastern University, Fort Lauderdale, and University of Central Florida, Orlando, modeled after University of California Irvine's iMedEd Initiative (Gillum and Chiplock, 2014), helped health profession faculty collaborate and connect across the disciplines to develop ways to use mobile devices to access accurate medical information. Librarians were instrumental in this collaboration as advocates for learning and decision-making. As noted in table 2.2, a librarian may be authorized by both the library and the outside group to participate as an embedded librarian (Andrews, 2015) in multiple ongoing projects and roles within the outside group, such as a key committee member or frequent guest lecturer, curriculum development, strategic planning, and continuing education for outside organization. In the UC Irvine initiative, the librarians brought various health profession faculty together, both creating and leading an embedded librarian project.

Librarians have worked together with IT security, vendors and authentication issues, and clinical directors to facilitate access to library resources and medical literature. LibGuides, library websites, tutorials, and workshops have helped medical professionals develop the use of mobile devices in the operating room, patient rooms, and clinics, increasing the opportunity to reach evidence-based decisions about patient care and drug information. These sustainable and strategic partnerships, with a librarian who collaborates with the outside group to create and develop mutual projects related to the educational process or success of the outside team, demonstrate deeper levels of librarian engagement and embeddedness (see table 2.2).

Tan and Maggio published an article in 2013 that explored more roles for clinical medical librarians embedded in patient care teams. They examined roles held by six Canadian medical librarians and one from the United States. Roles included researcher, teacher, content manager (creating a virtual library customized for patient needs), and patient advocate. The study discussed a very important characteristic gained by clinical health teams by adding an embedded librarian to the mix: the cognitive diversity of adding a knowledge or information expert to the teams. The librarian was more emotionally detached from patient care than the rest of the team, and able to offer a valuable evidence-based perspective for this team. The librarian was also able to actively observe how expert searching, content management, and teaching research skills resulted in better patient care and cost effectiveness for their clinics. Librarians embedded in the teams were able to save the time of the clinician, support decisions, and increase library visibility within the organization (Tan and Maggio, 2013).

Another example of different, more externally oriented embedded librarian practice was undertaken by the Welch Medical Library at Johns Hopkins University in 2013 (Welch, 2017). Welch librarians provided an embedded informationist service staffing model, assigned to provide information services within assigned departments of their users rather than the library. This staffing model was designed to bring the librarians to the users at the point of need for information with a digital library collection accessed by mobile devices or at locations close to their users' offices. This model brings an important question: Now that library resources can be accessed from anywhere, why are we staying in the library?

Embedded Special Librarians

A report by David Shumaker, published by the Special Libraries Association (SLA), describes different models of embedded librarianship. This report contains excellent characteristics and recommendations for embedded librarian programs, including the ability to relate well to others, to "build alliances and communication with customer management" (2009: 7). His report includes information on embedded librarians in non-profits, for-profits, and government agencies. He studied law librarians who analyzed their firm's information needs and created a content repository and database to assist the lawyers in their research. The report also describes librarians working within government agencies, outside of the library, with different titles related to information analysis. The report found embedded librarians working in most special library sectors. Successful programs were defined as having high customer demand for librarian information services.

Shumaker further advises in an *Information Today* article that librarians need to "get out of the library and get into the business" (Shumaker, 2012: 2). He recommends that librarians find new ways to relate to their users, learn more about the parent organization, get included in teams outside the library walls, and build new relationships. He advises librarians to take ownership in the information-related assignments on teams, to be the expert in this area. The 2009 report also discusses the need for administrative and library staff support, and a plan to assess the readiness of the library staff to undertake an embedded librarian staffing model, as well as funding and the need for staff cohesiveness.

Embedded School Librarians

Buffy Hamilton has authored numerous presentations depicting roles of embedded school librarians. A 2013 presentation for the American Library Association (ALA) Tech Source describes best practices for creating learning partnerships and relationships. She is a strong advocate for using emerging technology and social media to enhance and create a social learning experience within educational interests. This experience of learning together brings the partners together in a collaborative way that stimulates creative teaching and learning strategies. This perspective discusses librarians as content creators as well as creators of communities of learners.

An interesting article by Cordell from 2012 discusses an embedded school librarian "cultivating a network of learning partnerships around the globe to teach students of all ages the art of photography and digital storytelling" (Cordell, 2012: 8). She recommends using social networking to connect to national and international learning partners, integrating librarians into each other's educational programs. Her article also describes using technology tools such as Skype to virtually connect with libraries and learning communities.

⑥ Emerging Roles for Embedded Librarians

Common denominators for roles in all of these programs include emerging embedded librarian roles as content creators, catalysts, advocates for learning and decision-making, social learners, and knowledge/information experts. Reference and instruction services help users learn not only what resources are offered through libraries, but also the impact of librarians as they serve user needs for information. Embedded librarians provide personal services to users and can better provide these services if they have the opportunity to mingle with these users, and learn about their communities to create content that is valued by these communities. Emerging technology tools can allow solo librarians to virtually leave their library and expand the reach of their information services as well.

Educational and technology trends have created new opportunities for librarians to realize changes in their roles and how they serve their user communities. Librarians have learned creative ways to use their knowledge and skills—creating content and adapting to the changing needs of diverse users and learning communities. These adaptive qualities and skills that are necessary for embedded librarians facilitate change and find learning opportunities. Brian Mathews wrote about these new opportunities as he blogged about the need for adding change literacy to the list of literacies to accompany information literacy in 2014—"the ability to anticipate, create, adapt, and deal with change (in the broadest since) as a vital fluency for people today" (Mathews, 2014).

⑥ Key Points

Embedded librarianship has evolved organically as librarians have developed collaborative relationships with their communities. As information-seeking behaviors changed with technology, librarians found new partnerships that valued the unique skills and knowledge they brought to the table. The integrated teaching partner librarian role helped promote information literacy for users of all types of libraries. Inspirational articles that describe emerging roles for embedded librarians in different types of libraries were also covered in this chapter.

- Librarians have seen opportunities for new partnerships with rapidly changing technology and educational trends.
- A new level of integration beyond blended or liaison librarianship has evolved, especially as librarians left traditional supporting roles for embedded librarianship.
- All types of libraries are incorporating embedded librarianship into their service models. Examples are provided of academic, public, health sciences, special, and school librarians.
- Emerging roles for embedded librarians utilize content creation and new technologies and involve teaching and collaborative skills.

The next chapter will discuss how to assess readiness for change by librarians, libraries, and their communities to an embedded model of librarianship, using a commonly used business analysis model.

ⓖ References

ACRL (Association of College and Research Libraries). 2000. *Information Literacy Competency Standards for Higher Education.* American Library Association. http://www.ala.org/acrl/standards/informationliteracycompetency.

ACRL (Association of College and Research Libraries). 2007. *Standards for Proficiencies for Instruction Librarians and Coordinators.* American Library Association. http://www.ala.org/acrl/standards/profstandards.

ACRL (Association of College and Research Libraries). 2011. *Standards for Libraries in Higher Education.* American Library Association. http://www.ala.org/acrl/standards/standardslibraries.

ACRL (Association of College and Research Libraries). 2015. *Framework for Information Literacy for Higher Education.* American Library Association. http://www.ala.org/acrl/sites/ala.org.acrl/files/content/issues/infolit/Framework_ILHE.pdf.

ACRL (Association of College and Research Libraries). 2017. *Roles and Strengths of Teaching Librarians.* American Library Association. April 28, 2017. http://www.ala.org/acrl/standards/teachinglibrarians.

ACRL Roundtable on Technology and Change in Academic Libraries. 2006. "Changing Roles of Academic and Research Libraries." Association of College and Research Libraries (ACRL), November 2–3, 2006. http://www.ala.org/acrl/issues/value/changingroles.

Alvarez, Barbara. 2014. "Embedded Business Librarianship in 5 Steps." *Public Libraries Online,* December 2014. http://publiclibrariesonline.org/2014/12/embedded-business-librarianship-in-5-steps/.

Anderson, Dean, and Linda A. Anderson. 2010. *What Is Transformation, and Why Is It So Hard to Manage?* Change Leader's Network. http://www.beingfirst.com/resource-center/pdf/SR_WhatIsTransformation_v3_101006.pdf.

Andrews, Carl R. 2015. "Embedded Librarian Ideas: Best Practices Explored and Redefined." *International Journal of Educational Organization and Leadership* 22, no. 2: 1–14. http://academicworks.cuny.edu/cgi/viewcontent.cgi?article=1002&context=bx_pubs.

Becker, Cheryl. 2012. "A New Kind of Librarian." *A Life in Libraries* (blog). July 15, 2012. https://cherylbecker.wordpress.com/2012/07/15/a-new-kind-of-librarian/.

Bell, Steven. 2016. "What Do You Know about Instructional Designers? From the Bell Tower." *Library Journal,* May 12, 2016. http://lj.libraryjournal.com/2016/05/opinion/steven-bell/what-do-you-know-about-instructional-designers-from-the-bell-tower/.

Bell, Steven J., and John Shank. 2004. "The Blended Librarian: A Blueprint for Redefining the Teaching and Learning Role of Academic Librarians." *College & Research Libraries News* 65, no. 7: 372–75. http://crln.acrl.org/content/65/7/372.full.pdf.

Black, Lindsay, and Darra Ballance. 2013. "Teaching Evidence-Based Practice in the Hospital and the Library: Two Different Groups, One Course." *Medical Reference Services Quarterly* 32, no. 1 (January–March): 100–10. https://doi.org/10.1080/02763869.3013.749143.

Brandes, Susan, Karen Wells, and Margaret Bandy. 2013. "Invite Yourself to the Table: Librarian Contributions to the Electronic Medical Record." *Medical Reference Services Quarterly* 32, no. 3 (July–September): 358–64. https://doi.org/10.1080/02763869.2013.807087.

Church-Duran, Jennifer. 2017. "Distinctive Roles: Engagement, Innovation and the Liaison Model." *portal: Libraries and the Academy* 17, no. 2: 257–71. *Project Muse.* https://www.press.jhu.edu/journals/portal_libraries_and_the_academy/portal_pre_print/articles/17.2church.pdf.

Cooper, I. Diane, and Janet A. Crum. 2013. "New Activities and Changing Roles of Health Science Librarians: A Systematic Review, 1990–2012." *Journal of the Medical Library Association* 101, no. 4 (October): 268–77. https://doi.org/10.3163/1536-5050.4.008.

Cordell, Diane. 2012. "Skype and the Embedded Librarian." *Library Technology Reports* 48, no. 2: 8–11.

Drewes, Kathy, and Nadine Hoffman. 2010. "Academic Embedded Librarianship: An Introduction." *Public Services Quarterly* 6: 75–82. https://doi.org/10.1080/15228959.2010.498773.

Gillum, Shalu, and Amanda Chiplock. 2014. "How to Build Successful iPad Programs in Health Science Libraries: A Tale of Two Libraries." *Journal of Electronic Resources in Medical Libraries* 11, no. 1: 29–38. http://www.tandfonline.com/doi/abs/10.1080/15424065.2014.876580?src=recsys&journalCode=werm20.

Haglund, Lotta, and Per Olsson. 2008. "The Impact on University Libraries of Changes in Information Behavior among Academic Researchers: A Multiple Case Study." *Journal of Academic Librarianship* 34, no. 1: 52–59. http://citeseerx.ist.psu.edu/viewdoc/download?doi=10.1.1.453.6484&rep=rep1&type=pdf.

Hamilton, Buffy J. 2013. "Taking Embedded Librarianship to the Next Level: Action Steps and Practices." *Buffy J. Hamilton* (blog). October 31, 2013. https://buffyjhamilton.wordpress.com/tag/embedded-librarianship/.

Hovious, Amanda. 2013. "The Importance of Being Blended." *Designer Librarian* (blog). January 28, 2013. https://designerlibrarian.wordpress.com/2013/01/28/the-importance-of-being-blended/.

Jaguszewski, Janice M., and Karen Williams. 2013. "New Roles for New Times: Transforming Liaison Roles in Research Libraries." Association of Research Libraries. http://www.arl.org/component/content/article/6/2893.

Kolowich, Steve. 2010. "Libraries Make It Personal." *Inside Higher Ed*, September 28, 2010. https://www.insidehighered.com/news/2010/09/28/librarians.

Mathews, Brian. 2014. "ACRL: If We Are Putting Everything on the Table—How about 'Change Literacy' Too?" *The Ubiquitous Librarian* (blog). *Chronicle of Higher Education* March 10, 2014. http://chronicle.com/blognetwork/theubiquitouslibrarian/2014/03/10/acrl-if-we-are-putting-everything-on-the-table-how-about-change-literacy-too/.

Radniecki, Tara. 2013. "Study on Emerging Technologies Librarians: How a New Library Position and Its Competencies Are Evolving to Meet the Technology and Information Needs of Libraries and Their Patrons." IFLA WLIC 2013, Singapore. http://library.ifla.org/134/1/152-radniecki-en.pdf.

Raimondo, Paula G., Ryan L. Harris, Michele Nance, and Everly D. Brown. 2014. "Health Literacy and Consent Forms: Librarians Support Research on Human Subjects." *Journal of the Medical Library Association* 102, no. 1 (January): 5–8. https://doi.org/10.3163/1536-5050.102.1.003.

Shumaker, David. 2009. *Models of Embedded Librarianship: Final Report*. Special Libraries Association. http://hq.sla.org/pdfs/embeddedlibrarianshipfinalrptrev.pdf.

———. 2012. "Embedded Librarians in Special Libraries." *Information Today* 29, no. 7: 1–4. http://www.infotoday.com/it/jul12/Shumaker—Embedded-Librarians-in-Special-Libraries.shtml.

Sullivan, Brian T., and Karen L. Porter. 2016. "From One-Shot Sessions to Embedded Librarian: Lessons Learned over Seven Years of Successful Faculty-Librarian Collaboration." *College & Research Libraries News* 77, no. 1: 34–37. http://crln.acrl.org/content/77/1/34.full.

Tan, Maria C., and Lauren A. Maggio. 2013. "Expert Searcher, Teacher, Content Manager, and Patient Advocate: An Exploratory Study of Clinical Librarian Roles." *Journal of Medical Library Association* 101, no. 1 (January): 63–72. https://doi.org/10.3163/1536-5050.101.1010.

Tarver, Talicia, Dixie A. Jones, Mararia Adams, and Alejandro Garcia. 2013. "The Librarian's Role in Linking Patients to Their Personal Health Data and Contextual Information." *Medical Reference Services Quarterly* 32, no. 4: 459–67. https://doi.org/10.1080/002763869.2013/837730.

Tennant, Michele R., T. Cataldo, P. Sherwill-Navarro, and R. Jesano. 2006. "Evaluation of a Liaison Librarian Program: Client and Liaison Perspectives." *Journal of the Medical Librarian Association* 94, no. 4 (October): 402–4. *CINAHL Complete*, EBSCO*host*. http://eds.a.ebsco host.com/eds/pdfviewer/pdfviewer?sid=c8dce9ff-d8b2-41c3-85a1-c83926dc8828%40 sessionmgr4010&vid=7&hid=4211.

Turner, Arlee, Bernadette Welch, and Sue Reynolds. 2013. "Learning Spaces in Academic Libraries—A Review of the Evolving Trends." *Australian Academic and Research Libraries* 44, no. 4: 226–34. http://www.tandfonline.com/doi/pdf/10.1080/00048623.2013.857383.

Vassilakaki, Evgenia, and Valentini Moniarou-Papaconstantinou. 2015. "A Systematic Literature Review Informing Library and Information Professionals' Emerging Roles." *New Library World* 116, no. 1–2: 37–66. https://doi.org/10.1108/NLW-05-2014-0060.

Welch Medical Library. 2017. "The Welch Library Embedded-Informationist Program." William H. Welch Medical Library, Johns Hopkins University School of Medicine. http://welch.jhmi .edu/welchone/The-Welch-Library-Embedded-Informationist-Program.

Williams, Karen. 2009. "A Framework for Articulating New Library Roles." *Research Library Issues: A Bimonthly Report from ARL, CNI, and SPARC* 265 (2009): 3–8.

🌀 Further Reading

Kavanaugh, Jill R., Kristelle Lavalee, and Anna Miller. 2018. "The Role of Embedded Librarians in Educational Health Resources: Two Case Studies." *Journal of Consumer Health on the Internet* 22, no. 1: 72–79. https://doi.org/10.1080/15398285.2018.1415592.

Shank, John D., and Steven Bell. 2011. "Blended Librarianship: [Re]envisioning the Role of Librarian as Educator in the Digital Information Age." *Reference & User Services Quarterly* 51 no. 2: 105–10. https://i.slcc.edu/internalaudit/docs/teaching-become-blended-librarianship.pdf.

Tyckoson, David. 2003. "On the Desirableness of Personal Relations between Librarians and Readers: The Past and Future of Reference Service." *Reference Services Review* 31, no. 1: 12–16. https://doi.org/10.1108/00907320310460834.

SWOT

Analyzing Your Organization

The beginning is the most important part of the work.
—PLATO

> **IN THIS CHAPTER**

▷ Understanding what a SWOT analysis is and its role in developing an embedded librarianship program

▷ Creating a SWOT analysis of the library with examples from four different types of libraries

▷ Using the SWOT Analysis Worksheet 1

THIS CHAPTER WILL SERVE AS A GUIDE as you take your first steps in creating a strategy for embedded librarianship. You will need to gain more knowledge of the organization you plan to embed as well as acquire a new type of competency for working with people outside your library's organizational culture. Analyzing this new culture outside your library will help you learn about its basic nature, goals, and challenges, preparing you to undertake the work ahead. Once the decision is made to begin an embedded partnership with the outside group, the librarian may be uncertain where to begin and how to assist the new group. As discussed at the beginning of this book, you will need to "mingle with the reader" (Green, 1876). Until becoming part of the outside organization, the librarian may presume, somewhat erroneously, to know where help is needed. An emotional detachment and broad perspective is needed to see clearly where and in what areas to begin the embedded program. You will also need to assess your library's readiness for integration with this outside group.

A clear understanding of your library is the first step in planning any embedded librarianship program. According to Germano and Stretch-Stephenson, "Strategic plans are developed and executed by businesses in order to chart a course toward an idealized future destination for the organization. Normally, this means aspiring to become an industry leader or niche holder by increasing market share, developing customer loyalty, penetrating new markets or some other defined goal" (2012: 71). Meaningful goals that add value to patron experiences may be established by using SWOT analysis, a best practice in developing a strategic plan for both non-profit and for-profit enterprises. An example of an academic library using this tool for strategic planning may be found at the University of Mississippi—in the *UM 2020 Library Strategic Plan* (University of Mississippi Libraries, 2010). The UM Library plan paralleled the university strategic planning process in matching the library "mission, vision and core values" and plan structure/language to those of the host institution, and also in performing a self-evaluation of library services. You will need to have a clear picture of not only your perspective of your library's services, programs, and resources, but also your users' view of your library. Examining both the library and the group targeted for the embedded librarian program is another best practice for first steps in identifying goals and objectives for the librarian. A SWOT analysis of your organization is an important beginning to any plans you may hope to undertake.

What Is SWOT Analysis?

SWOT analysis is a powerful tool commonly used in business, especially when a company is planning to expand into a new market. SWOT is an acronym for strengths, weaknesses, opportunities, and threats. The origin of SWOT analysis is not confirmed in the business literature, but many attribute its development to both the Harvard Business School in the 1950s and Albert Humphrey of Stanford in the 1960s. Many libraries use SWOT analysis for developing their strategic plans. In the example used earlier by the University of Mississippi Library, the strategic planning document lists the strengths, weaknesses, opportunities, and threats and relates future goals to this analysis. Samples from UM 2020 that could be useful in planning an embedded librarian program include the following excerpts:

Strengths
- Skilled, flexible, and resourceful faculty and staff
- Culture of assessment for evidence-based decision making
- Extensive support for students both in person and at distance
- Collaborations, both on campus and regionally, to maximize funds and increase access to resources for students and faculty

Weaknesses
- Limited staff restricts the library's ability to expand services. . . .

Opportunities
- Increasing availability of digital information will enhance the libraries' ability to support extended services. . . .
- Increased outreach will enhance the library's ability to expand services and increase its role in the campus community

Threats
- Increasing student enrollment may create unmet needs
- Increasing variety in expectations for service pressure limited staff
- New campus-wide programs and areas of interest threaten the library's ability to provide high quality support with limited staffing and resources

(University of Mississippi Libraries, 2010)

When you use SWOT analysis to examine your library and the group into which you are hoping to embed, it can easily generate a vision and pathway to take your first steps in embedded librarianship.

⑨ Developing a SWOT Analysis for the Library

You will use the SWOT analysis framework to study your library as well as the organization you are hoping to embed. Your library may be a part of a larger organization you are studying, such as a library within a university, corporation, government, or news network. The organization you are observing may be directly connected to your library, such as a history department at a community college. You may also be looking at an organization completely unrelated to your library, such as a public librarian examining a popular charity organization in his or her community. In all these scenarios, you will be looking at two different cultures with different goals, issues, and languages. The SWOT analysis of both entities will outline both commonalities and differences that will be important to consider in planning your embedded strategy. You will want to align the strengths of your library with the needs of the group you plan to embed within. At the same time, you can align your library's resources with that group's threats to creatively disrupt their environment and help them address weaknesses or threats.

There are two sides to an effective SWOT analysis: internal and external. The internal side of the analysis looks at things you can control; the external side examines things outside your control. When you create a SWOT analysis of your library, you will be examining both sides to get a complete picture of your unique situation.

The strengths and weaknesses of your library include things you or the library administration can control, such as library services and your library collection. You will want to look at your library's strengths and weaknesses not only from the librarian point of view, but also from the perspective of your library users. You will also need to look at your library's strengths and weaknesses in the context of your external environment. What is freely available to your users? What makes the strengths of your library unique?

Opportunities and threats are external forces outside the control of the library, but they are related to your strengths and weaknesses. As you outline your library's strengths, you will develop a better awareness of opportunities. As you study your library's weaknesses, you can find perceived threats and better situate the library to improve upon its weaknesses and avoid future problems. For example, here are some introductory questions to consider:

1. Strengths—how does your library excel?
2. Weaknesses—where can your library improve?
3. Opportunities—what interesting trends can you see?
4. Threats—what barriers does your library face?

Strengths

The easiest way to begin a SWOT analysis of your library is to list all your current resources and services. Think about them in comparison to what is openly accessible to your users. What is available only at your library? How is your library already making a positive impact on your community? Are there some services or resources that are hidden gems for your users? Are you aware of services of which your users are not aware?

> ### EXAMPLE STRENGTHS
>
> - Librarians currently teach one-shot sessions in 65 percent of all English 1301 classes.
> - Library chat services are heavily used.
> - New database for pharmacy department includes most of the textbooks used by the department.

You will want to focus the strengths list you create in the context of the group into which you plan to integrate these same services or resources. Following are some example scenarios for your consideration.

Strengths Scenario A: Public Library

Library A is a public library within a small town that holds an annual community fundraiser walk for the American Heart Association. The library director is interested in somehow embedding the library into this event. Here are some strengths the director can list:

- The library website has a page dedicated to excellent consumer health resources with both subscription and open access resources.
- The library's social media page has a large number of followers.
- The library is located on the annual fund-raiser walk route.

Strengths Scenario B: Health Sciences Library

Library B is a health sciences library at a large university that is starting a nursing RN-to-BSN program and a PhD nursing degree. The librarian liaison to the nursing department is interested in becoming an embedded librarian in both new degree programs. Strengths for this library include the following:

- The library purchases four major databases for nursing including CINAHL Complete and has a subscription clinical drug database.
- The library purchase plan includes purchasing nursing textbooks for the library Reserves collection.
- The library has a subscription to a citation software program, and this software company provides excellent training modules online.

Scenario C: Community College Library

Library C is a branch library for a community college in an urban area, one of six campus libraries with a shared online collection and identical library services. The library manager is interested in embedding the library into the college psychology department. Following are the strengths for this library:

- The college library services information literacy team has just completed the creation of brief, generic modules for the research process including Choosing a Topic, Plagiarism and Citing, Finding Articles and Finding Books, and E-books. All the tutorials include a short quiz at the end that can be submitted for a grade.
- The college has a subscription to LibGuides, and there is a subject guide about researching psychology topics that is linked from the library home page.
- This branch library has a large print psychology collection in both reference and circulating books.

Scenario D: Hospital Library

Library D is a hospital library for a large pediatrics hospital. The solo librarian is interested in embedding the library into clinical rounds for the hospital pediatric residents program. This library has the following strengths:

- The hospital library has a website linked from the hospital home page and a web page in the hospital's intranet site.
- This library has a strong interlibrary loan program.
- Library services include managing the hospital continuing education program.

Weaknesses

The weaknesses of your library include your perceptions as well as how outsiders view your library. You may list library services or resources you cannot provide now that you have observed as available at other libraries with better funding. It may be part of a wish list already created in case the library budget has a surplus at the end of the fiscal year. It is also important to view weaknesses with an objective perspective. Your users may have completely different impressions of what are considered to be the weaknesses of your library. Their list of the library's weaknesses may include a need for services that they are not aware your library actually provides. When you list the library's weaknesses, you will also need to consider these misconceptions as well as the realistic weaknesses that exist at your library. Let's go back to the four scenarios and discuss some sample weaknesses, keeping in context the groups with which these libraries hope to become integrated.

Scenario A: Public Library

The public library director who hopes to embed the library into the fund-raiser walk activity lists the following weaknesses in the SWOT analysis:

- The library budget has recently been cut 10 percent.
- The community's webmaster is leaving for another position in two weeks, and the library director will not be able to make changes to the library website during the

resulting replacement webmaster hiring period. This time frame will overlap with the community fund-raiser event.

- The library consumer health print collection has a very small and somewhat outdated health reference and circulating print book section.

Scenario B: Health Sciences Library

The health sciences library liaison to the university nursing program does not have similar staffing or funding issues to Library A, but lists the following weaknesses:

- The past interactions between the health sciences library liaison and the nursing department have only included a handout included in the nursing students' registration packet with a link to the library home page, which includes a list of nursing databases and a short orientation session during the first week of classes.
- Only one nursing faculty member has requested a library instruction session for a core curriculum class assignment on a research paper in the past academic year. The professor divides the single instruction session time into two parts: one taught by the library liaison and one taught by someone from the university writing lab.
- One of the most outspoken professors in the nursing department recently wrote a letter to the health sciences library director and complained bitterly about the weeding of the print nursing collection journals from the periodicals shelves, which duplicated the online subscription nursing journals collection, to create a larger group study area in the library.

Scenario C: Community College Library

The branch manager for the community college library has a completely different list of weaknesses to list:

- This community college library branch has only two full-time librarians—including the branch manager, who also has administrative duties—who currently teach all the information literacy sessions at their campus.
- The other full-time librarian on this campus is a recent hire with only three months of experience in librarianship.
- Psychology classes are offered at two of the community college campus branches, including this one. The librarian who created the Psychology Research LibGuide left the college for another position eight months ago, and this LibGuide is currently an orphan with no assigned author. It also has not been updated in ten months.

Scenario D: Hospital Library

Library D has some similar issues to the other libraries. Weaknesses listed include the following:

- The hospital librarian is new not only to this hospital, but also to the area.
- The librarian whom the new librarian replaced was very unhappy about running the continuing education program and burned some bridges before leaving for other employment. The hospital was in danger of losing its library altogether due to damaged relationships with key stakeholders.

- Funding has been cut, limiting the number of database subscriptions available. In addition, although the interlibrary loan program is well established, the library budget limits fulfilling requests to those lending libraries who reciprocally charge a very small fee.

Opportunities

Discovering useful opportunities for your library will come from a combination of the knowledge of current trends and tools as well as how a library reacts to perceived weaknesses and threats. Weaknesses can be turned into opportunities, for example. Opportunities can also be identified as you create a list of your library's strengths. You will ideally also need to talk extensively with a friendly person who is already a part of the organization you hope to embed as your ideas for opportunities are only coming from your point of view. Look for opportunities that increase the visibility of your library and have low overhead costs. You may have already discovered some hidden opportunities in our four scenarios.

Scenario A: Public Library

Even without speaking directly to the American Heart Association in the public library's community, the library director may already see some opportunities such as the following list:

- The local American Heart Association in the community does not currently have a social media presence.
- The event fund-raiser chair called and asked to post some flyers at the public library. The library director has consented to post the flyers and set up a time to meet with the chair to find out if the library can be of further help to the fund-raiser.
- The library director recently attended a health fair and saw several booths that advertised free mobile apps, which gave the director some ideas about including links to mobile apps on the library's web page of consumer health resources.

Scenario B: Health Sciences Library

The health sciences library nursing department liaison has the ability to turn the library's perceived weaknesses into opportunities in the following ways:

- The outspoken nursing faculty professor who protested the weeding project could become an advocate for increasing faculty awareness of the library nursing subscription databases.
- The liaison librarian could take an active role in acquiring the textbook lists from the faculty for all the nursing courses offered during the current semester to confirm that the Textbook Reserves collection is complete and communicate the availability to nursing faculty and their students.
- The library could track reference desk question statistics specifically associated with nursing students and communicate a need for library instruction sessions with courses with a research assignment with the faculty. The liaison could also contact faculty whose students are having difficulties with completing assignments and offer library instruction.

Scenario C: Community College Library

The community college library manager can also view the perceived weaknesses that were listed as new opportunities:

- The new librarian can set up an individual appointment with each psychology professor, virtual or face-to-face, as both an introduction to library resources and services and also a fact-finding mission to learn more about the information and instructional needs of the department.
- The new librarian can also adopt the orphan Psychology Research LibGuide and use the fact-finding appointments to get the professor's input on how to improve and update the information in this LibGuide.
- The librarians can set up a visit during the psychology departmental meeting to introduce the new online tutorials to the faculty and discuss ways to integrate these tutorials into the curriculum.

Scenario D: Hospital Library

The new hospital librarian has some wonderful opportunities available. The librarian also feels that the outlined weaknesses must be addressed in order to move forward effectively. These weaknesses can also be turned into opportunities as following:

- The new librarian can seek input for the hospital continuing education program by creating a survey for continuing education topics that also may highlight library services. A survey creates an opportunity to open communication with groups and repair damaged relationships.
- The hospital is almost finished constructing a new research center that will be affiliated with a large university health sciences division. Faculty are actively seeking grant funding from the NIH for research teams, which may include an embedded librarian team member. According to a 2013 article in the *Journal of the Medical Library Association*, research-embedded librarianship is a rapidly developing model of librarians embedded within research groups (Greyson et al., 2013). Opportunities include involvement for the duration of the research project and full partnering with colleagues outside the library walls.
- The hospital uses an online hospital records program that patients can use to view their hospital records. The librarian recently met the records administrator and is thinking about asking if the system can link out to PubMed on the internal side and MedlinePlus on the external side of the system software. The evidence-based health information approach to health care has created new opportunities for librarians to support practice with supporting research and care guidelines as well as consumer health outreach services (Dorsett, 2014). The librarian sees an opportunity to embed with the hospital patient education and services information team, which surprisingly does not have an information specialist–type role at this time.

Threats

Threats for any embedded librarian program universally include staffing and budget concerns, including the rising costs of library resources. Concerns about cuts in these areas are commonly shared by all types of libraries. As mentioned earlier in this chapter, threats are external factors, outside the control of the librarian. Following are a list of threats perceived by the four scenarios.

Scenario A: Public Library

The public library director has several threats for concern:

- If the community cut the library budget last year, will there be more cuts in the future?
- The library needs to replace outdated consumer health materials, but will it be able to afford to continually update this part of the collection?
- Will the new webmaster reduce the library web presence on the community website?

Scenario B: Health Sciences Library

The health sciences library nursing liaison librarian has a strong awareness of some threats that could be viewed as opportunities as well:

- The nursing department is hiring many new full-time and adjunct professors who will teach online courses for the new BSN program. These new teaching faculty members are located all over the state. How can the library compete with other libraries across the state?
- How will the liaison communicate effectively with these professors from all over the state?
- Due to the outspoken nursing professor opposed to the library weeding project, there is a perception that the library is getting rid of its print resources to become an internet café.

Scenario C: Community College Library

The community college library branch manager is a part of a very organized library services team, with extensively coordinated operations and services. Threats include the following:

- If the library branch manager pursues an embedded librarian pilot for the psychology department, can this effort be opposed by the rest of the library services team or the leadership or administration?
- Will the library leadership be willing to let a new librarian with no previous LibGuides training assume ownership of the orphan LibGuide?
- This branch of the college just opened last fall and has a lower enrollment than the other campuses. Will the new librarian be placed at a busier campus library, leaving only the branch manager to handle all the campus library instruction requests, and will efforts toward embedded librarianship create too many requests to fulfill?

Scenario D: Hospital Library

The hospital librarian has a different variety of threats, mainly caused by the actions of the predecessor librarian. Here is a list of the threats the new librarian is encountering:

- If the librarian's efforts are not successful, could the hospital library be in danger of closing?
- Could the new research center's affiliation with the neighboring university cause the doctors to use the university library services to replace the hospital librarian?
- Could the informational needs for the new research center be so numerous that the solo librarian is unable to help it?

ⓖ SWOT Analysis Worksheet 1

The SWOT Analysis Worksheet 1 (see the textbox) was created to guide librarians with a specific embedded librarianship project through an assessment of their organization. You may want to start with a simple table to brainstorm some ideas for your SWOT analysis before you begin working your way through the first worksheet. An example of a draft SWOT analysis for a hospital librarian who is planning how to embed a research team is shown in table 3.1.

Table 3.1. Hospital Library SWOT Draft Analysis—to Embed a Research Team

	POSITIVE ASPECTS IN ACHIEVING GOALS	NEGATIVE ISSUES FOR ACHIEVING GOALS
Internal Values: Within Your Control	Strengths • Well-trained library staff • Relevant collection of databases • Librarian worked with one of the research scientists last year on library database funding • Librarian attended workshop on NIH grants and will be able to help research team with the grant proposal	Weaknesses • Time: Only one librarian with circulation staff—may cause the librarian to be unavailable at times • Librarian is intimidated about working with major research scientists
External Values: Outside Your Control	Opportunities • Research team leader approached librarian with request to help with literature review for the grant proposal	Threats • Library funding and justification for maintaining a hospital library is always a challenge at annual budget planning meetings

Now that you have completed this chapter, you have taken your first step in creating your strategic plan for embedded librarianship. In order to put theory into practice, a SWOT Worksheet 1 has been provided. Use this worksheet to reflect on the strengths, weaknesses, opportunities, and threats that pertain to the library where you work. The completed worksheet may be valuable in discussing goals with administration and forming initial strategies for an embedded program. Using the format of the table provided, table 3.1 on this page, next create a draft SWOT analysis.

SWOT ANALYSIS WORKSHEET 1:
YOUR ORGANIZATION

Strengths: What are the biggest strengths of your organization (the one you plan to embed)?

- Why are you interested in becoming an embedded librarian for *this* organization?
- Do you or does the library already have long-term partnering relationships with this group of people?
- Do you have a personal interest in the mission of this organization? List library services frequented by users for this type of organization.
- List library resources that you hope to use as an embedded librarian.
- Does your library have any *new* services or resources to offer?

Weaknesses: What gaps do you observe in your organization's resources?

- Do users from the organization display a gap in their knowledge about library resources selected for them?
- Is the organization heavily involved with research but seemingly lacking in expertise in using library sources?
- Does the library have access to tools, such as LibGuides, that may be of use to this organization? What gaps do you observe in your library's resources?
- Is the collection development for this type of organization supporting its information needs?
- Are there databases that the library budget cannot afford alone needed to support this group?
- Is the library staffed so that a librarian may periodically leave to help the organization?

Opportunities: Where do you see a need for an embedded librarian within your organization?

- Is the organization aware of library services and resources available?
- When did the library last reach out to this group?
- How do the library and organization communicate goals?
- Do you see gaps in the organization that could be helped by the skills of a librarian?
- How skilled are the researchers within the organization?
- Has the organization ever worked with a library partner?
- Does this group have knowledge of librarian skills and what will be brought to the table?

Threats: With what issues is your organization dealing?

- If it is an academic or health sciences department, is an accreditation visit happening soon?
- How has the current budget affected works as an organization?
- How is the organization dealing with different issues?
- Is there any current threat to the library's resources?
- Are budget or staffing cuts imminent?
- How is the library advocating for value and value-added services?
- How does the library make collection development decisions?

◎ Key Points

This chapter has discussed how to begin your embedded librarianship project by examining your library in the context of the organization you wish to embed using a SWOT analysis framework. It is important to look at the SWOT analysis with detachment. Looking at the big picture—how the library matches the mission of its parent organization, how the embedded target group views the library, and how the work of the librarians match user needs—will steer the group planning the embedded librarian program in the right direction. Consider thoughtfully the following points:

- You have completed a thorough reflection of the library as an organization using the SWOT Analysis Worksheet. This work will serve as a starting point on examining your organization's strengths, weaknesses, opportunities, and threats.
- Looking at the big picture at threats outside your control and weaknesses within your control helped form ideas that can be transformed into action by assessing your organization's strengths and opportunities.
- You have examined how your perceptions of the library organization's SWOT analysis may differ from those who work outside your library.

After brainstorming using table 3.1 and reflecting on your thoughtful results in SWOT Analysis Worksheet 1, you are now ready to look at the most important component that will be the key to your success—your librarian competencies and personal skill sets.

◎ References

Dorsett, Rebecca. 2014. "Outreach Services in Healthcare Libraries: Perceptions and Impacts." *Health Information & Libraries Journal* 31, no. 1. http://onlinelibrary.wiley.com/doi/10.1111/hir.12055/pdf.

Germano, Michael A., and Shirley M. Stretch-Stephenson. 2012. "Strategic Value Planning for Libraries." *Bottom Line* 25, no. 2: 71–88. https://doi.org/10.1108/08880451211256405.

Green, Samuel S. 1876. "Personal Relations between Librarians and Readers." *American Library Journal* 1, no. 1: 74–81.

Greyson, Devon, Soleil Surette, Liz Dennett, and Trish Chatterley. 2013. "'You're Just One of the Group When You're Embedded': Report from a Mixed-Method Investigation of the Research-Embedded Health Librarian Experience." *Journal of the Medical Library Association* 101, no. 4 (October): 287–97. https:// doi.org/10.3163/1536-5050.101.4.010.

University of Mississippi Libraries. 2010. *UM 2020 Library Strategic Plan.* University of Mississippi Libraries. http://www.libraries.olemiss.edu/uml/administration/strategic-plan.

◎ Further Reading

Dewey, Barbara I. 2004. "The Embedded Librarian: Strategic Campus Collaborations." *Resource Sharing & Information Networks* 17, no. 1–2: 5–17. https://doi.org/10.1300/J121v17n01_02.

MindTools. 2011. "SWOT Analysis: Discover New Opportunities, Manage and Eliminate Threats." SWOT Analysis. http://www.mindtools.com/pages/article/newtmc_05.htm.

Wichita State University Libraries. 2014. *University Libraries Strategic Plan, 2015–2017.* https://libraries.wichita.edu/ablah/images/files/ULStrategicPlan2015-2017.pdf.

CHAPTER 4

Analyzing Your Professional Skill Sets and Competencies

WHILE THE SWOT ANALYSIS used in the last chapter was all about the library and the organization you hope to embed, this chapter is all about you and your abilities, skills, knowledge base, and competencies. Analyzing your proficiencies objectively using the same SWOT framework is an essential step toward developing a successful strategy for any embedded librarian program. An effective self-analysis of professional abilities should also include input from others outside the library. For example, an instruction librarian needs to have a clear perception of his or her teaching skills to develop a clear picture of proficiencies and deficits. Assessing the instruction session by peers, students, or faculty will help the librarian complete an accurate SWOT analysis. The other key part of this self-analysis is a careful reflection of how you as a librarian view librarian identity and roles.

Tools for Evaluation

There are several standards in librarianship that can be used as tools in evaluating your skill sets. The ACRL *Standards for Proficiencies for Instruction Librarians and Coordinators* is an excellent point of reference as it lists "skills needed to be excellent teachers . . . and to foster collaborations necessary to create and improve information literacy programs" (ACRL, 2007). These proficiencies are applicable to librarians who work in other types of libraries as well. The Special Libraries Association has a similar document, *Competencies for Information Professionals of the 21st Century*, which lists professional, personal, and core competencies. The personal competencies are especially applicable to all types of librarians as they

> represent a set of attitudes, skills and values that enable practitioners to work effectively and contribute positively to their organizations, clients, and profession. These competencies range from being strong communicators . . . to remaining flexible and positive in an ever-changing environment. (SLA, 2003)

In other words, self-examination will include not only skills, but also personality and values. This examination will inspire ideas that are unique to your professional style, especially as interpreted in the context of how you will fit into the organization outside the library. ACRL revised the 2007 *Standards for Proficiencies for Instruction Librarians and Coordinators* to reflect the need for examining the roles librarians play in the context of the outside organization and to describe the strengths that librarians bring to the table. Areas may be identified for additional training and professional or personal growth.

ACRL *12 CORE PROFICIENCIES FOR INSTRUCTION LIBRARIANS AND COORDINATORS*

1. Administrative skills
2. Assessment and evaluation skills
3. Communication skills
4. Curriculum knowledge
5. Information literacy integration skills
6. Instructional design skills
7. Leadership skills
8. Planning skills
9. Presentation skills
10. Promotion skills
11. Subject expertise
12. Teaching skills

(ACRL, 2007)

Roles and Strengths of Teaching Librarians

- Advocate
- Coordinator
- Instructional Designer
- Lifelong Learner
- Leader
- Teacher
- Teaching Partner

From *Roles and Strengths of Teaching Librarians*, adopted by ACRL 28 April 2017 (ACRL, 2017)

Librarian Identities in Crisis

Before beginning a SWOT self-analysis, spend time reflecting on the concept of the librarian identity and how you visualize it fitting into the embedded librarian role. Think about how you talk about your work and the impact you have as a librarian. Most job titles do not convey clearly the type of job responsibilities you may have. For example, what is your job title? Following is a list of some of the current titles used by librarians:

- Librarian
- Reference librarian
- Informationist
- Information services librarian
- Information specialist
- Educational technologist
- Instruction librarian
- Education librarian
- Subject librarian
- Medical librarian
- Clinical librarian

There is a large body of academic literature that discusses the librarian identity crisis and librarian stereotypes. Pop culture and cinema have created diverse librarian characters that further perpetuate this identity mystique. Nicole Pagowsky's blog *Librarian Wardrobe* "documents, organizes and makes accessible" photos submitted by librarians (2014). Librarians submit their own photos to the blog in order to represent different images of librarians. The blog serves as a visual confirmation that a stereotype for librarians is no longer easy to define. Pagowsky has further developed this concept in a book she recently published with Miriam Rigby, *The Librarian Stereotype: Deconstructing Perceptions & Presentations of Information Work* (2014). This book discusses perceptions of librarians and how they are stereotyped, describing the impact made by librarians in spite of these stereotypes.

How libraries have changed has also affected librarian identity. An example is the historical change from closed stacks to open stacks in American libraries. In the past, librarians were viewed as gatekeepers who preserved the collections kept hidden from the reader and maintained as archives of information. When collections became accessible in open stacks, the reader was free to browse a collection without needing to ask the librarian for assistance. The cards in the card catalogs during that time often included librarian notes that referred the reader to other resources in order to find more information. These card catalog notes were created by librarians so that even the reader who was reluctant to ask for assistance could find these additional resources. With the evolution of technology and access to more information for free online, the relevance of libraries has come into question and created more questions about the public's perceptions of librarians. Professional associations have worked vigorously to advocate the importance of libraries for communities, schools, and corporations. Much literature has been written to advocate for libraries, but not much advocacy has been created about the need for professional librarians. How do you answer the following questions?

- What do librarians do?
- Why do librarians matter?
- If information is everywhere, why are we still using the library?

REFLECTIVE EXERCISE: WHAT MAKES YOU TICK?

1. List three recent experiences where you experienced pure job-love. What were you doing?
2. What part of your job would you do even if you were not paid to do it?
3. What is the easiest part of your job?
4. Do you look forward to working with a favorite group of people within your organization?
5. Has anyone recently thanked you for your professional assistance?

⊚ Roles of Librarians

In this chapter, you have been asked to reflect on questions of identity that librarians encounter. If what you do can be easily communicated, it will be easier to develop new and transformative relationships within the organization as a whole. Understanding the role of an embedded librarian within an organization is a threshold concept that is essential to any librarian's success. Once this core concept is understood, a shift in understanding librarianship occurs. It is a paradigm shift, valuing not only libraries, but librarians, which is unforgettable and allows the learner to make connections with the concept of librarianship. There is a transition that will result not only in a changed approach to reference transactions but also in integrative relationships with librarians. Once this concept is realized, the organization will advocate for librarians. Some organizations have moved embedded librarians into their offices and out of the library due to this transformative concept.

Preparation for a SWOT self-analysis must include listing the various roles you already play within your library as well as transferrable roles in the organization where you hope to be an embedded librarian. Create a list of the various committees that are served outside the library. Look at the outside organization's committees for areas that would be a great fit for you. Is there a technology, curriculum, or training committee that would match your capabilities? If serving on outside committees, what contributions (no matter how small) have you made? Don't just sit on a committee and hope you will not get the question, "Why are you here?" Analyze why a librarian is serving on these outside committees and be prepared to respond to such questions/comments. Be proactive and volunteer for special assignments.

Another role to examine is participation in campus or organizational initiatives, innovations, or programs. Perhaps you have participated in creating new library services or selecting new library resources. What role did you play in implementing these changes within the library that could be applied to effect positive changes outside the library? Skills unique to librarians include the ability to see connections to support decision makers. Librarians are regular collaborators in knowledge production. The basic proficiencies that are central to librarianship include organizing, classifying, and facilitating access to information. Knowledge of intellectual freedom, privacy, access, copyright, licensing, and learning facilitation are special and unique qualities also native to librarians. For example, librarians may be involved in providing access to homework help for local schools at your public library, or they may be creating pathfinders for local community organizations linked from their local website.

SAMPLE: SWOT ANALYSIS—LIBRARIAN SELF-DISCLOSURE ANALYSIS

1. **Strengths:** What are your greatest skills as a librarian; what comes naturally and easily for you?
   I love teaching, both planning and implementation. I have very good technology skills. I am also good at building rapport with students and faculty. I am willing to accept change and try new things. I believe in continuous improvement. I have a growth mind-set.

2. **Strengths:** What progress have you made to integrate library services and resources into your organization so far? List any accomplishments you have as an embedded librarian in the past or at previous organizations.
   We have a variety of resources in different formats with several access points available. We also provide several access points for help such as video tutorials and chat reference. We have created a good classroom environment for active learning with new furniture and technology. We have also created customized instruction sessions using such tools like LibGuides.

3. **Weaknesses:** What are your fears associated with embedded librarianship? Do you have any perceived educational or professional development gaps? Do you wish you had training to help you be successful?
   There are a few of the specialized databases that we do not use regularly that I am not as familiar with. I think the navigation of our website and portal are a weakness also.

4. **Weaknesses:** Has anything happened to make you more cautious about initiating an embedded librarian program at your organization? Do you have any confidence issues that need to be resolved before you move forward?
   I have no confidence issues.

5. **Opportunities:** What programs would it be easiest to embed and why?
   Our English composition and public speaking courses would be the easiest to embed in because they definitely have a research component in each class.

(continued)

6. **Opportunities:** Where do you see the greatest need for an embedded librarian at your institution?

   Our online students do not receive the same level of service and instruction as our f2f (face-to-face) students.

7. **Opportunity or threat:** What instructional or fun technologies are you most familiar with using?

   I am familiar with LibGuides, LibraryH3lp, Google Drive Suite, Smartboard, Snagit, Articulate, Bubbl.us, Prezi, and Diigo. I am learning Captivate, Canvas (LMS), and Google Hangouts.

8. **Opportunity or threat 2:** What tools do you have at your institution? What free tools are available?

   All of the above (Q7) from our institution or free. Some other technology I want to try out is Quizlet, GoAnimate, Issue, and Thinglink. All are free.

9. **Threat:** What do you consider to be your biggest obstacle to being a successfully embedded librarian?

   Communicating with our online instructors will be my biggest obstacle. Most of our online instructors are adjuncts, and our institution's communication system is not dynamic enough to provide adequate service.

Technology and Literacy

Technology has changed how organizations access information. Most decision makers have daily informational activities that can produce information overload. A common concern encountered by the stakeholders in any organization as well as those involved in instruction is how to effectively evaluate information, a daily activity for most librarians. Librarians can bring a type of cognitive diversity into any discussion about information as they may have a completely different perspective on how to evaluate information that is based on professional skills and knowledge of the information cycle. Librarians can also bring an emotional detachment to the discussion, such as finding information for patient care or teaching children with learning disabilities. The librarian has the advantage of only being involved in the dissemination of information, without the emotional attachment to the patient or child.

Evaluating information, information literacy, and critical thinking skills are central to core competencies for librarians in general, and for embedded librarians in particular. As information has become more accessible through technology, new skills in digital, health, and financial literacy have evolved into preferred job requirements for different types of librarians. Brian Mathews recently suggested that change literacy, "the ability to anticipate, create, adapt and deal with change (in the broadest sense) as a vital fluency for people today," should be added to the list of skills important today as well (2014). Librarians have been working at the forefront for many years in the changing publishing and information access environments within their institutions and nationally. The profession has been the face of change for open access, new pedagogy, collection migration, e-book licensing, social learning spaces, and makerspaces. Librarians have embraced change in technology, shared learning processes, and the management of big data. This expertise is a significant asset to any group, especially those outside librarianship, who might benefit from an embedded librarian.

⑥ Librarian Personalities and Embedded Librarianship

Reflecting on your core competencies and capabilities is very important in preparing your personal SWOT analysis, and an awareness of personality is also a critical aspect in this type of evaluation. One of the major misconceptions librarians have about embedded librarians is that it's necessary to be an extrovert to be successful. This idea is usually connected to a perception that the librarian must sell the library or market the library in order to be an accomplished embedded librarian.

As a librarian becomes embedded within an organization, he or she creates integrated relationships and connections with many different personalities. The librarian may be a change agent or the one who documents the evidence behind the decisions to make changes. There is no common personality type required to do this work, except for a sincere willingness to help others. A librarian may model or suggest changes in pedagogy, such as adding a small-group work or flipping the classroom, but there is no need to sell or lead the change. The librarian must engage in conversations about pedagogy with those outside the library and work together to determine if change should be implemented. The cultural and cognitive diversity offered by the librarian will assist the group more than possessing a selected personality type.

Misconceptions about the personalities of embedded librarians are connected to current trends in leadership. Librarians regularly attend conferences and staff development sessions on leadership. Being a good leader is very important, but there is a need for training in developing collaborative working relationships, teamwork, and generating trust. The most important personality traits for embedded librarianship include these three important components. Librarians who work well as members of a team and create a culture of trust and dependability can play valuable and critical roles within the organizations outside their libraries. Trust is a necessary element for meaningful communication. Ideas you communicate that meet the needs of the outside organization will gain more leverage than ideas that the organization does not understand. Trust is a necessary part of any honest negotiation.

You may have to overcome internal confidence problems or strive for personal growth as you work to become an embedded librarian. It is vital to learn as much as possible about the culture of the larger organization in order to bridge this obstacle in your self-perception. Most librarians have no idea what a difference they can make within this new, larger group. At the beginning, it may seem difficult to know how to be of assistance to this group, but you must learn to trust your instincts and skills. For this reason, it is very important to know as much as possible about yourself and what you bring to the table. The unique communication system used by the organization outside the library may seem intimidating, but the more you are immersed in the whole organization, the more successful the experience.

It's not necessary to become an expert in a new field outside librarianship either. For example, a medical librarian does not need an additional medically related degree to be an embedded librarian for a surgical care unit. The librarian just needs to understand the members of the outside organization and ask thorough reference interview questions. As strengths are listed in the SWOT self-analysis, a clearer picture will develop of all the skills and qualities a competent librarian has to offer as well as a renewed confidence and self-esteem needed to move forward.

Along with understanding your proficiencies and personality, it's important to analyze individual motivations. Various personality preference quizzes can be used, such as the Myers-Briggs MBTI test, which offers insights by the classification of personality preferences into sixteen distinct types. According to Myers and McCaulley, "If people differ systematically in what they perceive and in how they reach conclusions, then it is only reasonable for them to differ correspondingly in their interests, reactions, values, motivations, and skills" (1985: 3). In other words, the different ways people develop perceptions are related to how they interpret or make judgments or reach conclusions. These personality types are often used in career profiles or helping to select a new career. Examples of career profiles may include both extroverted and introverted personalities—both types work well in embedded librarianship. Creating an awareness of how you work best is the key to success.

As you examine both internal and external components in the personal SWOT analysis, look at how you are motivated by intrinsic or extrinsic work rewards. Extrinsic rewards include those motivating factors that are outside our control, such as earning an award or being promoted. Intrinsic rewards are those that are internally motivating. For example, some may prefer to create a spreadsheet to analyze thoroughly all the factors involved in making a decision. Others may prefer to create checklists and tabulate all the tasks accomplished at work. Some librarians may find influencing change or making a difference at work to be the most rewarding part of the job, while others feel most rewarded at work by being a part of organizational change, including the relationships created within the process. More details about the various motivational types are described in the following textbox. Examining what is the most rewarding part of the job will provide important insights into what motivates you.

MOTIVATIONAL TYPES

Go-Getter

The go-getter enjoys a challenge and dislikes micro-management. This motivational type strives for excellence and improvement. Go-getters respond well to goal setting and may be perceived as insensitive to the feelings of others.

Caregiver

The caregiver enjoys belonging to a group and nurturing others. This motivational type seeks varied social activities and invites advice from supervisors. Caregivers avoid conflict and may sacrifice goals to maintain strong relationships.

Influencer

The influencer embraces change and shaping the opinions of a group. This motivational type works well alone or with other power brokers. Influencers may be too forceful in voicing opinions but may positively affect confidence in making group decisions.

You are now ready to proceed with the librarian SWOT analysis, using the SWOT Analysis Worksheet 2. Consider previous roles both within the library and also the current relationship established with the new group you have targeted for the embedded librarianship project. The framework will include the same categories as the analysis performed earlier in chapter 3:

- Strengths
- Weaknesses
- Opportunities
- Threats

As strengths and opportunities are assessed, consider carefully which opportunities may increase your visibility as well as the visibility of the library within the organization. If information is available everywhere, why use the library? The library's accomplishments or the accomplishments of the outside organization may be fragmented. How can an embedded librarian help create connections or collaborations with other groups? How does a librarian generate trust and shared responsibilities with librarian colleagues? How have librarians already worked with individuals from the outside organization? As opportunities are identified, think about identifying unique opportunities with shared goals between the library and the outside organization.

Weaknesses and threats on your list may be perceived or real. Addressing both may be accomplished by requesting more training, attending staff development sessions or conferences. Be honest with yourself and list any concerns or fears you may have at this time. Do you know anyone who already works as an embedded librarian? You may want to talk to your supervisor about acquiring a mentor or partnering with another librarian. The most common weakness listed by librarians in this SWOT analysis: librarians do not know how to get started. Many librarians join outside committees only to approach these meetings with great apprehension. The process of completing both SWOT analyses in chapters 3 and 4 is a good beginning to developing confidence and constructing a strategy for moving forward.

After completing both the library SWOT Worksheet 1 from chapter 3 and the self-analysis SWOT Worksheet 2 in this chapter, you should thoroughly compare and analyze the results. The analysis may have identified some great ideas for embedded librarianship and new librarian roles within the outside organization.

SWOT ANALYSIS WORKSHEET 2: LIBRARIAN SELF-DISCLOSURE ANALYSIS

Strengths:

- What are your greatest skills as a librarian?
- What comes naturally and easily for you?

Strengths:

- What progress have you made to integrate library services and resources into your organization so far?
- List any accomplishments you have as an embedded librarian in the past or at previous organizations.

Weaknesses:

- What are your fears associated with embedded librarianship?
- Do you have any perceived educational or professional development gaps?
- Do you wish you had training to help you be successful? If so, what training do you believe you need? Has anything happened to make you more cautious about initiating an embedded librarian program at your organization?
- Do you have any confidence issues that need to be resolved before you move forward?

Opportunities:

- What would be the easiest, small change you can make to move forward as an embedded librarian at your organization?
- Which tools, resources, and/or services do you feel are essential that your organization learn?
- If you could not fail, what would you do differently at your organization?
- What technology tools or apps do you have available at your organization?

Threats:

- What do you think is your biggest obstacle to becoming embedded in your organization?
- What scares you the most about embedded librarianship at your organization?
- What is the worst thing that could happen if you begin to work as an embedded librarian?
- If there is a budgetary or staffing issue holding you back, are there some creative ways to overcome these problems?
- How will you react if you are told libraries are no longer relevant in today's information age?

⑥ Key Points

This chapter focused on the keys to your success as an embedded librarian: your proficiencies and your personality. The results from both the SWOT analyses from chapters 3 and 4 will be used to develop your action plan in chapter 6. Following are the most important points to understand about chapter 4:

- Be aware of misconceptions about personality traits needed to be a successfully embedded librarian. It's important to understand fully how you perceive yourself in the context of the group you hope to embed with a sincere desire to be of service to this outside group.
- As past accomplishments are examined, you may gain insights on what motivates you and how you define success. Perceptions, whether real or imagined, are based on how you process information, your personality type, and what motivates you.
- Librarians are intricately involved in change, including digital, health, media, financial and information literacy, as an integral part of operating libraries. Whether or not you have been aware of your role in these literacy issues, the library profession has been at the forefront of emerging technology, scholarly communication, community building, and how information is disseminated to scholars and the public.
- Use SWOT analysis to perform a self-examination of your perceptions, expectations, fears, and self-imposed limitations. Reflect carefully upon what inspires you to take action. Be mindful of tools, creative solutions, and the ways threats may be turned into opportunities.

After finishing your SWOT analysis, you will be ready to look at ideas for beginning work as an embedded librarian. Look at the results of the self-analysis in the context not only of your library, but also the outside organization you hope to embed. If you already work closely with a member of this outside group, consider discussing with this person the opportunities you have listed. You may need this perspective to clearly view the outside group using the group's point of view. The next chapter will describe the importance of reflection and visualizing the embedded librarian role within the organization before creating a strategic plan.

⑥ References

ACRL (Association of College and Research Libraries). 2007. *Standards for Proficiencies for Instruction Librarians and Coordinators.* American Library Association. Last modified June 24, 2007. http://www.ala.org/acrl/standards/profstandards.

ACRL (Association of College and Research Libraries). 2017. *Roles and Strengths of Teaching Librarians.* American Library Association. April 28, 2017. http://www.ala.org/acrl/standards/teachinglibrarians.

Mathews, Brian. 2014. "ACRL: If We Are Putting Everything on the Table—How about 'Change Literacy' Too?" *The Ubiquitous Librarian* (blog). *Chronicle of Higher Education.* March 10, 2014. http://chronicle.com/blognetwork/theubiquitouslibrarian/2014/03/10/acrl-if-we-are-putting-everything-on-the-table-how-about-change-literacy-too/.

Myers, Isabel Briggs, and Mary H. McCaulley. 1985. *Manual: A Guide to the Development and Use of the Myers-Briggs Type Indicator.* Palo Alto, CA: Consulting Psychologists Press.

Pagowsky, Nicole. 2014. "Librarian Wardrobe." *Librarian Wardrobe*. Tumblr. September 14, 2014. http://librarianwardrobe.com/post/31537416158/new-shoes-for-fall-systems-librarian-jewish.

Pagowsky, Nicole, and Miriam E. Rigby. 2014. *The Librarian Stereotype: Deconstructing Perceptions & Presentations of Information Work*. Chicago: Association of College and Research Libraries.

SLA (Special Libraries Association). 2003. *Competencies for Information Professionals of the 21st Century*. Last modified June 2003. http://www.sla.org/about-sla/competencies/.

◎ Further Reading

Alvarez, Barbara A. 2017. "Embed with Business: Taking Your Library into the Business World." *American Libraries* 48, no. 1–2: 44–48.

Beard, David. 2018. "Morning Mediawire: The Pulitzer-laden Researcher Embedded in the Post Newsroom." *Poynter*, April 24, 2018. https://www.poynter.org/news/morning-mediawire-pulitzer-laden-researcher-embedded-post-newsroom.

Brunvand, Amy. 2017. "Sustainability on the Other Side of the Stacks." *American Libraries*, May 22, 2017. https://americanlibrariesmagazine.org/blogs/the-scoop/sustainability-side-stacks/.

Greyson, Devon, Soleil Surette, Liz Dennett, and Trish Chatterley. 2013. "You're Just One of the Group When You're Embedded: Report from a Mixed-Method Investigation of the Research-Embedded Health Librarian Experience." *Journal of the Medical Library Association* 101, no. 4 (October): 287–97. https://doi.org/10.3163/1536-5050.101.4.010.

Hackman, Dawn E., Marcia J. Francis, Erika Johnson, Annie Nickum, and Kelly Thormodson. 2017. "Creating a Role for Embedded Librarians within an Active Learning Environment." *Medical Reference Services Quarterly* 36, no. 4 (October–December): 334–47. https://doi.org/10.1080/02763869.2017.1369280.

Pentland, Courtney. 2014. "An Attitude of Empowerment." *School Library Monthly* 30, no. 4: 31–32.

CHAPTER 5

Reflection

Matching Your Personality to an Embedded Role within the Organization

MOST PROFESSIONAL ORGANIZATIONS and workplaces offer highly structured periods of orientation to new employees. The new employee is introduced to the mission and values of the new environment as well as its organizational leaders and procedures. Many organizations appoint a mentor for the new employee to help this person learn both the formal and informal means of communicating, making changes in procedures, and navigating effectively in the new environment. The organization may have a unique jargon, such as using acronyms or local naming conventions, which can be confusing to a new employee. An embedded librarian will need to design his or her own orientation into the new organization. Since the librarian may be breaking new ground, it is highly unlikely that a formal orientation plan will be in place for this librarian. The embedded librarian will need to plan how best to assimilate into this new culture and pick one or several mentors for assistance in this process.

In chapter 4, the roles and proficiencies of the librarian were analyzed with the intent of planning how to best serve the outside organization's needs as an embedded librarian. The next consideration in the planning process is analyzing the personality of the librarian and how he or she will fit into the embedded organization. A recent article by Schofield (2013) states this consideration very well in context: "People differ in their personalities, attitudes, and values, and an understanding of our individual personality is profoundly important in maximizing our happiness and productivity at work." Most librarians who have served on hiring committees for various types of libraries are familiar with the concept of cultural fit. It is an important concept to consider whenever adding a newly hired person to any staff. Finding a new employee who values the goals and mission of the hiring organization is important to the success of any organization or business. For example, if an academic library is focused on student success initiatives, it will look for a job candidate who values education and the impact it can make on individual lives. Most embedded librarians are successful because of the beliefs and values they share with members of the embedded organization.

There are many personality types in each organization: introverted or extroverted, as well as competitive or welcoming. If all of these different personality types embrace the vision and values of the organization, it can become a powerful and successful group that ably meets the vision set forth by its administration. Most workplaces also embrace diversity in the work environment as well. The employees don't have to have the same personality or background in order to fit well together as a culture. Think of the workplace as a flock of geese: not all can lead, and most fly in a pattern that resembles a V shape. The ones in the back who honk and drive the others forward are as important as the ones in the front who lead. Group work in outside organizations is similar to group work in libraries in personality matching and collaboration techniques. Take time to reflect on successful group interactions in your work history and compare them to groups in the outside organization.

Cultural Assimilation

A clear understanding of the librarian's own personality is invaluable to become assimilated in the new culture. Take time to research and learn about this new culture and also reflect on how your personality will fit into this new group of people. Any librarian with solid reference interview and research skills will find it relatively easy to construct an orientation into the embedded organization. Reflection on how your personality and work ethic will fit into the organization must be included as well. Find a library-friendly ally and ask for assistance in learning more about the organization, or simply focus on assisting a single person. For example, a reference librarian at a major university may choose to work closely with an English composition professor who regularly assigns a library research project. The librarian can inquire about the curriculum, the syllabus, and how well students succeed in the assignment, and then offer ideas and value-added services. As the professor and librarian begin to partner and experience improved student outcomes, the professor will assist the librarian by recommending that others partner with this librarian too. The librarian may be able to add more library resources to the professor's syllabus and bring up discussions within the department about linking to library resources from the syllabus or online classroom management system or integrating with library instruction sessions or the librarian's online learning objects. The professor may begin to list the librarian as a guest lecturer in the class syllabus, and the librarian may be asked to attend departmental meetings and faculty retreats.

UNPREDICTED GROWTH IN AN EMBEDDED DEPARTMENT

A health sciences librarian worked closely with pharmacy faculty who taught a drug literature course. The librarian would come by the professor's office at the beginning of each semester and help construct the syllabus, adding links to library databases, articles, e-books, and LibGuides. During the second semester that the librarian helped the professor, a professor from the same department stopped by, and the librarian and the professor shared how they worked together. The pharmacy professor championed the impact that their work had on students during the course. The second professor asked the librarian to stop by afterward. The second professor shared an office with a third professor, who overheard plans to have the librarian develop a new research project, and soon the librarian was now helping three professors. The librarian found that these professors shared the news about their new projects with the rest of the faculty, and the next day, two more pharmacy professors stopped by the library at different times, both asking to meet with the librarian to develop integrated research assignments. Soon the librarian was very busy helping five professors at the start of the year. These five faculty became librarian advocates and even asked the dean of the department if the librarian could have an office with regular office hours within the department.

⦿ Orientation

Although there is no set curriculum to a self-directed orientation, there are some standard elements that will be essential to your success as an embedded librarian. Keep in mind that there are some informational materials and resources that you can locate or consult without help, such as course descriptions in the course catalog, a website, or literature distributed by the organization, but it is important to know that you will need to use your reference interview skills to talk to people who work inside the organization to get the whole perspective needed to be successful.

Learning about the structure of the new organization is a critical part of embedded librarianship. Every organization has key decision makers, values, procedures, and

**SAMPLE SELF-ORIENTATION:
HISTORY DEPARTMENT EMBEDDED LIBRARIAN**

A community college librarian discusses becoming embedded within the history department with a history instructor, Dr. Smith. This instructor has requested help with creating reading lists for US HIST 1301 from the librarian and requests a library instruction session each semester in preparation for a research assignment. The librarian learns that Dr. Smith mentioned all the assistance provided each semester to the rest of the department, and the other instructors are interested in working more closely with the librarian as an embedded partner. The librarian prepares some preliminary questions before meeting with the rest of the department to ask the instructor. What questions would you prepare?

communication structures in place. Following is a list of important elements for the prospective embedded librarian to investigate; these should be easy to find using the organization's marketing resources:

- Mission statement of the organization
- Goals for the organization or each department
- Organizational chart
- History of the organization
- Administration contact information
- Forms to contact the organization
- Images that visually describe the organization online
- Annual or traditional events
- Annual reports and other outreach materials
- Social media

Review these elements and look for connections to embedded librarianship. In other words, look for opportunities where a talented librarian's skills could help achieve goals, where the mission statement for the library and the embedded organization overlap, or where an embedded librarian could improve communication or processes, or could contribute to the vision of the organization. Most traditional orientations review these elements to make the new employee feel welcomed and more comfortable with the new workplace. The embedded librarian should view these elements in a similar mind frame, looking for ways where a librarian's skill sets would be helpful and welcomed in the new organization. For example, a high school may offer an annual college fair each fall semester. The school librarian could volunteer to participate in the college fair by coordinating with the counseling department to assist with finding financial aid resources at the college fair. Often the counseling staff is busy running the fair and would appreciate having a trusted researcher available to research the answers to financial aid questions and offer other reference librarian assistance.

ANNUAL EVENTS

If you are planning to embed within a non-profit organization such as the American Diabetes Association in your area, take a look at the annual events offered in your area. Most annual events have a need for volunteers to help organize or work at the event. These events offer an excellent opportunity to get to know the members of the organization in a more informal setting. This opportunity is especially important if personal interests or beliefs are aligned with this annual event. These events offer multiple chances to network and get to know more about the organization, its leaders, and its stakeholders. Examples of embedded librarian work within a charity event may include any of the following:

- Marketing the event using library social media or posting information about the event at the library
- Staffing a table at the event with related information, such as Best Websites for Credible Diabetes Information, Diabetes Support Groups
- Creating a Diabetes LibGuide to be linked from the Annual Event web page for the American Diabetes Association

Most successful orientations are designed as a process rather than an event. Behaving as the newbie is a great way to get started. Do not hesitate to ask others for help in navigating the organization, physically or virtually. Introduce yourself, explain what you are trying to do, and ask for assistance. Be prepared to offer ideas and examples for embedding the organization. Always remember to learn the name of the person who provided assistance to you and take the time to visit briefly with him or her. A new employee is usually encouraged to ask for directions, and these questions will help you meet more members of the organization. If the organization uses acronyms or jargon new to you, ask for clarification. Effective communications will need to include the language of the embedded group. Getting to know all levels of staff is also critical to your success. Take care not to make assumptions about the roles others play in the organization. Taking time to speak with others and learn more about the culture is the first step in building new relationships within the new organization.

AVOIDING ASSUMPTIONS

A children's librarian at a public library was working hard to become embedded at a local elementary school. The librarian was able to work with the school librarian to coordinate ESL (English as a second language) literacy activities for interested parents. The librarian had noticed a friendly man who was not taking the classes who was usually hanging around the library front desk each time she arrived to lead the ESL activities. She usually invited him to participate, but the man declined. The librarian assumed the man was too embarrassed to join the activities. The same librarian stopped by to see the principal a few days later and discovered that he was the man she assumed was too shy to participate. She realized she had not bothered to introduce herself to him. Fortunately, he did not realize that she did not know his identity, and in the future, the librarian made sure never to assume she knew a new person's role within the organization.

Most organizations have formal leaders outlined in an organizational chart; however, there may be informal leaders or centers of influence that play a major role in the decision-making for the organization. It is important to have a clear understanding about the formal decision-making processes. Work to meet both formal and informal leaders and share your aspirations with them, offering support for their endeavors. A strong researcher can offer skilled support for evidence-based decisions. Although you may not work very closely with organizational leaders, familiarity with librarian skill sets and the library's resources or services is essential for embedded librarian success. Steer clear of any political situations and stay as neutral as possible. It is possible to listen carefully to both sides but avoid taking sides. Neutrality and bridging differences by bringing groups together is a much better tactic in the face of any political situation.

During the process of orientation, the new employee becomes mindful about the organization's expectations for the new employee. Most hiring committees discuss how a candidate's skills and personality will fit into existing teams. Discovering the role an embedded librarian will play within an outside organization is a similar process. The librarian will have some ideas derived from the SWOT analyses from the previous chapters or from library management/administration but can discover new roles by asking questions and learning more about the organization. Get to know the people who work there and set realistic goals as you learn more about what is important to them. Communicate clearly what you bring to the table within the embedded group. The librarian should be mindful that the people in the organization will be discussing the librarian's role, personality, skills, and ideas as a group as well. Always exercise caution in getting involved in any of the organization's office politics, and strive to remain neutral within the organization. For example, if a librarian in a university becomes aware of a group of faculty who are working in opposition to the department head, the prudent librarian should be careful not to align with either faction and carefully strive to maintain neutrality within the situation. Look for ways to strengthen alliances, facilitate connections, and foster new relationships.

Although the culture of an organization may seem to be an intangible concept, according to Edgar Schein, there are "anthropological models" (2010: 14) within culture that are easily identified and observed as a group. His book on organizational culture lists clues that fall under this type of category:

- Group behavioral customs or shared language—for example, do the professors within a department address each other by first names during meetings or more formally (Dr. Jones)? (Schein, 2010: 14)
- "Rules of the game"—for example, the shared processes or protocols that must be followed to accomplish things
- "Climate"—this clue may be observed by looking at the physical spaces or offices—are there many shared offices? Or does everyone have a private office? (Schein, 2010: 15)

An embedded librarian may observe different aspects of organizational culture, but will also need to discuss these observations with a trusted ally within the organization. For example, the school librarian may need to talk to the social studies teachers about the procedures used to make a change within the curriculum, again to avoid making erroneous assumptions. As the librarian becomes embedded within the social studies curriculum at that school, the librarian will be able to participate as a part of the group as new processes are developed. Until then, the librarian will need to ask questions and confirm how things are done within the group.

Librarians often have a secondary degree in the specialty area of the organization in which they hope to embed. Possessing a college degree or skills in the second specialty is useful and often makes it simpler to gain cultural ease in the organization. It is important to maintain the librarian role, in spite of the second specialty. The cultural diversity a librarian brings into any organizational culture should not be diluted by over-identifying within the specialty. For example, if a librarian has a bachelor's degree in biology and works in a corporate library at a pharmaceutical firm, the librarian should plan to embed the departments at the firm as a librarian, not a biologist. The librarian role brings value-added services and resources to these departments, and this cultural and cognitive diversity will aid in the librarian's efforts toward embedded librarianship.

When an embedded librarian worked within a university pharmacy department, she was invited to be a member of the pharmacy new programs committee. A new PhD program was in development, and one of the questions that the committee was charged to determine was the prerequisites for the first-year students in this program. Most of the committee members were licensed pharmacists, relatively new to academia. The value added by having an experienced academic librarian sit on this committee included the librarian's extensive knowledge of how benchmarking may be applied to develop new programs. She offered to benchmark other PhD programs for prerequisites—and later for open educational resources used in lieu of textbooks within the PhD curriculum. She also was able to answer questions about similar new PhD programs within the university plus questions about current applicable resources already provided by the library databases and e-book collection.

NAVIGATING COLLEGE OFFICE SPACES

Many college faculty office spaces have confusing, mazelike arrangements with room numbering systems that are difficult to understand. If arranged by department, the clerical workers often only serve the department heads and may not be able to guide a new person to a specific office. Luckily, most college faculty are very aware of problems with office room numbers or cubicle spaces and will help a librarian locate a professor's office. I have often stopped and asked a professor for assistance and ended my appointment by making two new connections instead of just the one I planned to meet. When asking for directions, always take the time to introduce yourself and tell faculty why you are meeting with the other professor. Learn their name, what courses they teach, how long they have worked at the college. Use time wisely to generate new relationships and let people know how a librarian can be of help to them and their work.

⊚ Effective Communication and Personalities

Communication is another essential element in any orientation process. Most organizations have formal and informal communication procedures, which may include specific acronyms or jargon for email subject headings or work teams. There may be email groups, a paper mailbox system, and protocol for telephoning or emailing as well as more informal processes to learn. Workers may communicate using only office equipment, or they may share personal cell numbers. It is important to inquire about joining the formal email groups and other formal forms of communication, but be patient about being included in such processes. Most librarians are not added to formal communications without having an organizational advocate or administrator involvement. The librarian may have to be satisfied initially with having important communications forwarded before being added to Listservs or other formal communication systems.

When initiating communication with people outside the library, strive to be a little more formal at first. If attending a meeting, wear a name badge and hand out business cards. Emails should include a formal signature that clearly identifies your title and contact information. Some librarians include a professional head-shot image so they can be easily identified. It helps to personalize librarian services and makes it easier for others to find the librarian when they enter the library. The librarian can brand him- or herself as the organization's personal librarian. Always remember to be respectful of other's needs; when telephoning a contact, inquire if it is a convenient time to talk.

While creating an embedded presence, it is important to work to find common ground for working together. Be mindful of how individuals impact others. Learning to communicate is experiential in nature. The librarian must learn from trial and error how to become a part of the new group.

The librarian should be very open about efforts to partner with the organization with all new contacts. Being honest and sincere will help generate trust and foster new relationships. The spirit of helpfulness that most librarians embody is readily welcomed and refreshing to the organization. The librarian should also be aware that many people don't know what librarians do, and you will need to be ready to explain your profession often as you start to embed the organization. Have a planned response that includes a topic to which they can relate and understand. For example, a common topic of how to evaluate information can be used as a part of your introduction. Most librarians are aware of the "CRAAP test" attributed to the University of California State, Chico's Meriam Library (see the following textbox), but many people outside librarianship have never heard about it. You can explain that librarians help people learn how to evaluate information or websites as a part of explaining their role within the organization. Most people have experienced information overload while researching information and express concern that they are relying on misinformation as a part of their regular digital activity. Most professors are concerned about their students finding credible information. Talking about a topic that interests many people during a self-introduction can help start a new conversation within the organization about the topic and the librarian's role as well.

THE CRAAP TEST CRITERIA FOR EVALUATING INFORMATION

- Currency: the timeliness of the information
- Relevancy: the importance of the information for your needs
- Authority: the source of the information
- Accuracy: the reliability, truthfulness, and correctness of the information
- Purpose: the reason the information exists

(Meriam Library, 2010)

In his book *Lead with a Story*, Smith (2012) describes in a very compelling narrative why storytelling is so important and appealing. Introducing yourself and describing how you hope to work as an embedded partner may be more effective if you can give real-life stories such as example scenarios that illustrate the librarian's impact on student success. These stories can help with getting people's attention, creating a memorable narrative, and sharing your vision of how you hope to help with their goals. Talking about teachable moments with students, sharing eye-opening anecdotes about the difficulties students have experienced in completing a research assignment—stories like these at an academic library are great ways to get conversations started about what you hope to contribute to the course.

Effective communication can be established by practicing a trial-and-error process within the organization. Being new to the organization and reminding others you are trying to learn will be useful as you become culturally acclimated. Seek feedback and advice from others in the organization and be respectful of their time and attention. For example, a medical librarian embedding in a surgical resident program may want to ask for feedback from the director of the program to learn if the librarian is meeting the expectations of the team.

Building new relationships and partnerships may be difficult at first as librarians may not be viewed as part of the team network. Learning about the needs of the team and helping to get work done accurately, easily, and in a professional manner is a great way to demonstrate your role within a new group. In the example above, the librarian may find surgical residents are having difficulty locating accurate information quickly in a clinical situation. The librarian may be able to recommend mobile apps to library databases or URLs to practice guidelines. Other recommended initial interactions recommended by Parker in his book about working in cross-functional teams include:

- Acting as ambassador for the team or the library—building support
- Coordinating tasks
- Scouting—seeking information needed by the team to complete key objectives
- Being accessible—making yourself easy to find and easy to talk to
- Focusing on their needs, not yours
- Being responsive
- Being credible

(Parker, 2003)

◉ Developing/Improving Social Skills

A librarian may have personal social limitations that could pose obstacles to being a successfully embedded librarian. Many people experience nervousness and fear of new social situations. They may dread small talk or trying to think of what to say when first meeting others. Social skills can be developed and practiced in order to feel better prepared for meeting new people. Good conversation is more thoughtful than precise. An awareness of body language and other nonverbal communication cues can also be helpful in new social experiences.

Even if a person feels awkward socially, practicing nonverbal conversation cues can convey a more confident attitude. Maintaining eye contact while speaking to others, a welcoming posture, and a friendly facial expression can help others feel welcomed and comfortable, even while feeling nervous or insecure. When entering a meeting room, notice how others have seated themselves. Don't assume a seat in the corner; sit next to someone and introduce yourself. A common error that librarians make when attending meetings with people from other departments is sitting together in a corner—failing to interact with other departments. Take risks and meet new people at each meeting attended. Set goals to meet several new people at each different meeting to practice good social skills. Observe people with excellent social skills and note what techniques are used to make others more comfortable.

A good strategy for most people seeking to elevate their comfort level in new social interactions is to play the host/hostess at the event. Welcome others and introduce people. Another great strategy is simply to compliment others' appearance in a friendly, professional manner. Other good opening comments include talking about the weather or a current event. Another conversation starter is simply asking others if they have worked at the organization for a long time. When introducing yourself, always take the opportunity to explain very briefly what you do and why you are attending the meeting/event. View yourself as a partner rather than assuming a supporting role. Be mindful of the impression made on these new partners.

Set specific goals, such as the number of people you hope to meet, or possibly plan to meet a specific person at the meeting/event. Be aware of defensive or off-putting body language, the volume of your voice, and the physical space maintained in groups. For example, a librarian colleague would habitually pull at her jacket lapels and hunch her shoulders while visiting with others in social situations, as if to physically shrink away from the group. Her colleague took her aside and talked to her about the message conveyed by this defensive posture. She made a conscious effort to change this habit and found people seemed friendlier to her. Another example: A young librarian made a great first impression but tended to punctuate his conversation with bursts of loud, nervous laughter that seemed rude, which made others uncomfortable. His supervisor took the time to discuss how the nervous laughter was affecting others' perception, and he was able to quickly make a change for the better.

When attending a meeting of the outside organization, take time to meet people and talk with them before and after the meeting. When meeting new people before a meeting or during an event, be sensitive to other groups. Two people talking intensely together may be discussing a private work matter and may not appreciate being interrupted. It is better to approach a group of three or more as well as other solo attendees. Be open about your personal interests or hobbies outside work. Be sensitive to how interested others are in the topics discussed and avoid monopolizing the conversation. Observe good social etiquette and be aware of projecting professionalism as well as approachability.

Feedback from trusted colleagues can be very useful in improving social skills. Ask a colleague or friend for input about both verbal and nonverbal conversation, and practice talking to new people as others observe. Practice will help alleviate nervousness, and it will be easier in time to enter new situations that may feel socially awkward. It is useful to know about nervous habits that may hinder best efforts toward cultural assimilation.

CONFIDENCE GROWTH

A librarian colleague who was working to become an embedded librarian in a key academic department was invited to join the department's curriculum committee. At the first meeting she did not sit at the conference table, choosing instead to sit in one of the extra chairs where the observing grad students also sat. She did not talk to anyone and confided later that she feared they would ask her to leave when they learned she was a librarian. The chair entered the room and as part of starting the meeting, introduced her and invited her to sit at the table. She moved to the conference table as requested.

During the meeting she was asked several questions about library services and resources, which she answered to the best of her ability. By the end of the meeting, she realized the committee actually needed her assistance to accomplish its goals. When she attended the meeting the second time a month later, she sat at the conference table. One of the attendees sat next to her and thanked her profusely for all the assistance she provided at the previous meeting. By the end of the semester, she was asked to chair a subgroup and was becoming more and more involved, even though she had a rough start at the beginning.

⊚ Key Points

This chapter discussed how the embedded librarian can work to assimilate the culture of the outside organization, becoming an embedded partner. The librarian should reflect carefully throughout this acculturation process to discover how his or her individual personality and skill sets will best fit into this new organization. The most important points of this chapter include the following:

- The librarian should work to create a cultural fit within the organization without losing the librarian's identity or getting involved in political situations.
- Learning informal and formal communication procedures, assimilating these processes into daily use, and meeting decision makers are essential components needed to establish new relationships within the organization.
- The librarian can improve social and communication skills with practice and trusted feedback.

During this chapter the librarian has been tasked with reflecting upon socialization within the group targeted for the embedded librarian program. The next chapter will help the librarian plan an effective strategy for becoming an embedded librarian within the outside organization.

⊚ References

Meriam Library. 2010. "Evaluating Information—Applying the CRAAP Test." Meriam Library. California State University, Chico. September 17, 2010. http://www.csuchico.edu/lins/handouts/eval_websites.pdf.

Parker, Glenn M. 2003. *Cross-Functional Teams: Working with Allies, Enemies, and Other Strangers.* 2nd ed. San Francisco: Wiley.

Schein, Edgar H. 2010. *Organizational Culture and Leadership.* 4th ed. San Francisco: Wiley.

Schofield, Kelly. 2013. "Cultural Fit in the Workplace: How Personality Affects Hiring and Teamwork." ERE Media. June 21, 2013. http://www.ere.net/2013/06/21/cultural-fit-in-the-workplace-how-personality-affects-hiring-and-teamwork/.

Smith, Paul. 2012. *Lead with a Story: A Guide to Crafting Business Narratives That Captivate, Convince, and Inspire.* New York: American Management Association.

⊚ Further Reading

Badia, Giovanna. 2012. "Relationships between Librarians and Faculty Still Need Further Investigation." *Evidence Based Library and Information Practice* 7, no. 3: 80–82. https://doi.org/10.18438/B8H90H.

Leeder, Kim. 2011a. "Collaborating with Faculty Part 1: A Five Step Program." *In the Library with a Lead Pipe* (blog). April 7, 2011. http://www.inthelibrarywiththeleadpipe.org/2011/collaborating-with-faculty-part-i-a-five-step-program/.

———. 2011b. "Collaborating with Faculty Part 2: What Our Partnerships Look Like." *In the Library with a Lead Pipe* (blog). July 13, 2011. http://www.inthelibrarywiththeleadpipe.org/2011/collaborating-with-faculty-pa.rt-2-what-our-partnerships-look-like/.

Sharma, Pramod, Kamal Kamar, and Parveen Babar. 2014. "Embedded Librarianship: Library Faculty Collaboration." *Journal of Library and Information Technology* 34, no. 6: 455–60. https://publications.drdo.gov.in/ojs/index.php/djlit/article/viewFile/7059/4702.

CHAPTER 6

Creating an Action Plan for an Embedded Program

EMBEDDED LIBRARIANS WITH CLEARLY outlined goals, timelines, and action items to match the process will see the clearest path to success. Since the partnering work may take the librarian away from usual duties within the library, it is important to be able to track and report progress to library administration, colleagues, stakeholders, and the partnering organization. Accountability, communication, and wise time management are vital for reaching the outcomes for any set of goals. This chapter will include tips and techniques for creating an effective action plan plus making the transition to an embedded role. It cannot be over-emphasized how important the action plan creation will be to partner with the organization that the librarian plans to embed. The goals must be transparent—easy to measure and communicate both how and why the outcomes are successful or unsuccessful. This transparency will also help other librarians follow these pathways to set up more embedded programs in the future.

Setting up the action plan with reasonable expectations and identifying the scope of the new project with the partner organization and library stakeholders will pave the way to good results. Following are the steps you will need to take for a goal-oriented action plan:

1. Fact-finding
2. Setting SMART goals
3. Checking goals for sustainability

⑥ Fact-Finding: Selecting Community Candidates for an Embedded Librarian Partnership

The first step after completing the SWOT analysis is fact-finding—a thorough reference interview with potential partners who already have expressed support and a need for the librarian's work; these are the library's champions. These candidates for partnership may be identified not only by librarians, but also by administration and circulation or public services staff. Regular library services users, active researchers who have already worked closely with a librarian, even community users who depend on the library for programming or resources may become active partners in an embedded program. Neutral questioning about the outside organization, including inquiries about new initiatives, changes in curriculum or prerequisites, new community services, new programs—any changes occurring in the organization—usually start conversations where librarians will find their services or skills are needed. This first step will identify these opportunities, beyond the librarian's SWOT analysis, and all the possible participants and stakeholders involved in any organizational changes. The librarian should try to interview several people from the department or organization outside the library and get different perspectives on possible opportunities for embedding a librarian. Continue interviewing people for three to six weeks to identify a clearly defined area as the starting point.

An excellent article by Brenda Dervin and Patricia Dewdney (1986) discusses the importance of neutral questioning in any reference interview, but it is particularly a key to identifying the first step in the goal-setting process. A common approach used in most reference interviews is to simply try to match library resources to user needs. This approach may be problematic for fact-finding as the librarian may unconsciously assume or anticipate what is needed by the user and completely miss a more pressing need for library services. Using questions that would solicit an answer of either yes, no, or maybe does not often help retrieve all the information needed to work with the interviewee. Open questioning—inviting the person to talk freely about his or her organization's challenges, problems, changes, opportunities, or weaknesses—can help both the librarian and the potential partner discuss where the librarian may be able to make a major contribution to this organization. Neutral questioning includes making sense of the informational needs as well as gaining an emotional intelligence or temperature taking of the user's needs. More closed questions may be used within the interview to help narrow down ideas or ask about more details, but the approach should be as neutral as possible, to have an exploratory conversation, not push instant solutions to the partner.

NEUTRAL QUESTIONING

If the librarian is unfamiliar with the neutral questioning approach, some sample questions or a sample script may be handy to use.

How to open the conversation:

- I heard the students in communication studies are having a poster presentation competition—could you tell me more about it?
- I was excited to hear about the new Sustainable Ag program—could you tell me more about what you are planning to do?
- I heard the English classes are now required to write a self-change essay—what kind of support do you need from the library?
- I have recently had several students ask questions about the new mathematics program—could you tell me more about it?

It is difficult to determine what direction the conversation will take, as this type of interview is highly situational, but the biggest tip is to avoid premature diagnosis, pushing services, or offering quick solutions. The librarian will need to take detailed and accurate notes, but avoid giving an easy answer during the process. Active listening and an effort to fully understand the organization from the eyes of the new partners may result in a new relationship, a new library program, and an embedded partnership.

Shumaker and Makins (2012) created several recommendations about successfully embedded partnerships; these included moving toward engagements with new partners that are strategic as well as tactical. The librarian may work within the embedded group to solve an information or services need; however, it is more effective to work together as partners to improve services or move toward the group mission. Also, the librarian should seek opportunities created by the interests of the organization members, rather than the librarian's interests or assumptions. It is important to listen carefully to uncover needs and develop a customized plan of how to best contribute within the embedded relationship.

Once the librarian has spent time talking to potential embedded partners and gathering facts, an initial set of goals may be created related to the organization's challenges. First, spend time writing a thorough report about these challenges or initiatives after each fact-finding interview to create an outline that includes organizational goals, partner goals, anticipated problems or perceived information gaps, and a list of participant partners. Meet with library stakeholders or administration to gather ideas on current and/or new library resources/services that may match the user's needs. Goals that are easier to attain and/or will create more visibility for the library should have top priority for any embedded librarian program. Goals that are easy to complete with efficient timelines help cement the new embedded librarian role and encourage the partners to work more closely together. Each goal may be classified in any of the following categories:

- Highly visible projects versus under-the-radar projects
- Projects or challenges that include several organizations such as campus-wide initiatives versus departmental or public program initiatives

- Goals with shorter time frames versus long-term projects
- Measurable, quantitative goals versus qualitative goals
- Expensive versus inexpensive projects
- Projects that will affect many people versus small-scale projects
- Goals that are labor intensive or detailed versus simpler projects

---

SAMPLE PROJECTS:
HIGHLY VISIBLE VERSUS UNDER THE RADAR

The Urban Libraries Council (2016) publishes descriptions of innovative projects. A highly visible project occurred in Minnesota where the St. Paul Public Library (2017) began an embedded racial equity partnership as a part of the city's strategic plan to address equity and inclusion. The library expanded collection development and provided information and resources using a LibGuide that encouraged citywide suggestions for future additions. This guide included information on economic disparities and provocative reading lists, such as a list of readings related to racism and civil rights. Initiating a project such as this one with national recognition creates visibility not only for the library but also for the city. The library could have supported this town initiative with simple collection development and programming in an under-the-radar-type effort, but it is a stronger partner by bringing visibility to the strategies of its community. The librarians spent time fact-finding, interviewing planners for this initiative to learn in-depth answers about the city's plans and aspirations. The librarians embedded themselves into the strategic plan, working with city partners to identify shared goals and objectives. The LibGuide and the expertise of the embedded librarians created new ways to develop critical conversations and invite community participation.

Campus-Wide Initiatives

An unconventional campus-wide initiative for embedded librarians was introduced at the ACRL 2017 Conference. Librarians from Dartmouth College Library embedded a campus-wide housing initiative, Moving Dartmouth Forward, with a shared goal of providing "more opportunities for intellectual engagement through social encounters among students, faculty, and staff." Librarians became "active and integral members of house communities," "establishing new faculty partnerships and collaborations with student life staff." Dartmouth librarians actively pursued fact-finding by attending campus initiative meetings and taking an active role in the planning and implementation process. The initiative start-up was hosted by the library, and student housing groups were paired with house librarians to support student success. Librarians interviewed student housing and student life to learn more about fail points for student retention and completion. New relationships with campus departments, faculty, and student groups were made, and the newly embedded librarians were able to create outreach and programming activities that met the goals of campus-wide groups (Barrett and Harding, 2017).

Short-Term versus Long-Term Projects

Short-term campus-wide projects are an excellent way to begin an embedded librarian program. In 2013, Purdue University librarians embedded into a short-term, campus-wide provost initiative for course redesign—"Instruction Matters: Purdue Academic Course Transformation (IMPACT)." The urgency and scalability of the project provided campus librarians an opportunity to begin conversations about embedding curricular design across all academic departments. Once the librarians learned about the provost's ideas, they began asking quality questions, interviewing department chairs and faculty, and discussing possibilities for embedding point-of-need resources into the online courses. Their fact-finding sessions identified critical thinking and information literacy student learning outcomes. Librarians worked on support teams to help integrate information literacy outcomes, created LibGuides to support courses, and assisted with instructional design modules within the learning management system. The embedded librarians serving on "IMPACT support teams . . . [exhibited] characteristics of both 'blended' and 'embedded' librarians" (Maybee, Down, and Riehle, 2013).

Another example of a short-term embedded librarian project is a technology adoption partnership, such as one in 2015 at the University at Buffalo (UB) Health Sciences Library mobile reference initiative. A technology initiative works well with outreach for embedded programs, and faculty early adopters are receptive to working together on these types of projects. It is important to center fact-finding interviews around the user experience in embedded technology programs. Liaison librarians experimented with iPads and Apple TVs for both instruction delivery and embedded services at UB, sharing what was learned with embedded departments (Stellrecht and Chiarella, 2015).

Long-term embedded projects are described throughout this book where librarians strive to become permanent partners in various areas such as instruction, curriculum and course development, community programs, and clinical settings. Both short- and long-term goals are useful for embedded programs. Baby steps can lead to long-range goals and new partnerships. The key component is finding that gap or information need using proficient reference interviewing skills where a librarian may make a major impact.

Measurable, Quantitative versus Qualitative Goals and Data

An excellent article by Lyon et al. (2015) includes descriptions of using both quantitative data and qualitative surveys to analyze librarian experiences and perceptions serving in clinical settings. The study also was used to indicate future training needs and librarian preparedness for embedding within point-of-need health environments. The study not only includes basic fact-finding in preparation for embedding the librarian within the clinical setting, but also describes the librarian reactions within the embedded role. The authors used various methodologies to gather quantitative and qualitative data to describe the embedded librarian role and perceptions about the role. These same methodologies could be used in a similar way to set embedded librarian goals and gather data within various types of libraries and embedded organizations. This article discusses the importance not only of searching for facts, but also learning about perceptions during the initial embedded librarian conversations. Examples of methods used include demographic surveys, qualitative testimonials, and a stress study, as well as training goals in librarianship and reference.

Small-Scale Projects versus Major Projects

Goal setting may also depend on the scale of the embedded project. Initial fact-finding should include questions about the size of the project and its impact on the embedded organization. Embedded librarian programs may be expensive or inexpensive, small scale or large scale within the mission of the organization, simple or labor intensive. Wu and Mi (2013) describe a range of embeddedness for health sciences librarians from small-scale to major projects. Small-scale embedded projects in the article included integrated course instruction ranging from a guest lecturer within one class session to a team teacher. These types of programs are easier to implement and may be useful if fact-finding indicates a reluctance from the new partners to devote a large chunk of time to an embedded partnership. A faculty member may want to try a smaller project to trial new steps before embarking on a larger-scale initiative.

Large-scale embedded goals included teaching within the health sciences curriculum, like embedded librarians who teach credit classes within the law core courses. Examples of embedded librarian courses within the curriculum include courses on the literature of the health sciences profession, such as a drug literature course or a nursing PhD course that introduces research methods for dissertation preparation. Additional labor-intensive goals include embedded clinical librarian and consumer health librarian roles as well as serving on a research team or becoming part of a community health organization team (Wu and Mi, 2013).

Setting SMART Goals

The next step in the process of creating a goal-oriented action plan is to set up your goals. There is much information available about setting SMART goals, that is, goals that are:

- Specific—not too complex or vague
- Measurable—easy to track and identify progress
- Attainable—able to achieve the goals within the timeline
- Realistic—relevant and mutually beneficial for both parties
- Time based—clearly defined milestones with sustainability

SMART goals were developed to help managers establish objectives and "their respective action plans" by George T. Doran (1981: 35). Writing and communicating these goals can be a daunting task for any project manager. The SMART goals acronym was developed to help establish quantifiable criteria for planning. Doran states that "the suggested acronym doesn't mean that every objective written will have all five criteria" (1981: 35). However, if the goals do meet all five elements, it does indicate that they are meaningful and attainable.

Specific Goals

The first letter in the SMART goals list—S—stands for specific goals that are appropriate and relevant. Broadly stated goals, such as "I plan to meet more faculty in the history department," have poor reliability in comparison to more specific goals—"I will identify the key faculty decision makers in the history department who design the research assignment for US History 1301." The appropriateness of a goal may be defined as one that matches both the values of the library as well as those of the group the librarian hopes to embed. If the librarian or the history faculty are not motivated to work with you to achieve a specific goal, it is not appropriate. The goal should also specifically be related to the higher priorities for both the library and the embedded department. For example, the library may want to show an increase in the number of instruction sessions and in the usage of its e-book collection. The history department may want students to use more scholarly sources in their research assignments and write better citations. A specific goal will define precisely what outcomes both departments wish to attain. Write a plan that includes the following elements:

- Who—Who will be involved in the embedded librarian program, both at the library and in the embedded department? Who are the stakeholders?
- What—What roles will the embedded librarian, library staff, the library director, and the people in the embedded department play in carrying out the action plan? What will be accomplished with this embedded partnership?
- Where—Where will the work of the program occur? In a classroom? Online or face-to-face?
- When—When will different steps in the action plan be scheduled? Will there be room in this timeline to make changes and allow the process to flow?
- How—How will the embedded department and librarian reach their shared goals?
- Why—Why does the department want to work with the librarian and the library? Why are their plans important to their departments?

Conversely, be cautious about concentrating on a single, specific goal. If you are fixated on attaining only one goal, that will result in an action plan that is so specific that the results are only sink or swim. There is greater value in establishing several specific goals that contribute and work together to design a solid embedded librarian action plan.

Measurable Goals

Creating goals that are measurable help you determine the success or failure of the embedded librarian program. Think carefully about how the success of the program will be measured and avoid creating a definition that is either too narrow or difficult. It is difficult to manage any project if you cannot measure its results. Well-written goals use phrases and sentences that are precise and easily explained. Select action verbs within the language of the goals thoughtfully. For example, the verbs "improve," "increase," "develop" are not easily quantifiable alone without adding standards such as how improved, how much something increased, or how something may be developed. If the library wants to measure an increase, for example, in instruction requests, a specific amount is better. The library could measure an increase by a percentage, by numbers of requests, or by the number of requests from the embedded department. The measurable goals may include a timeline with planned dates, data numbers, and statistics that indicate improvement toward reaching the shared vision between the departments.

Another important component in setting measurable goals is setting a baseline. For example, if the success will be measured using library instruction request statistics, take some time working with library administration and staff first to look for opportunities within the data already collected. Another baseline to establish in addition to library statistics involves time management. Spend time examining how much time is already spent on related tasks to help determine how long it will take to attain the goals for the embedded librarian project.

Attainable Goals

Goals may be challenging, but they also need to be possible to attain. This aspect of goal setting separates the dream goals from the achievable ones. It may be helpful to visualize what goals may be reachable and work from there to write new objectives. The embedded librarian may want to expand current services and will need to consider past librarian roles and support to be determine what may be accomplished. It is helpful to write goals using an action verb to ensure these goals focus on something that is attainable. Example verbs may include the words "complete," "investigate," "propose," "revise," "plan," and so forth.

Goals are also easier to achieve when broken into smaller tasks. The steps must include assignments that are within the scope of the embedded librarian's abilities and be generic enough so that other librarians could follow these steps too. The writing of attainable goals may be compared to choosing a topic for a research paper. If the topic is too broad, it is difficult to cover the topic well within the framework of the paper. If the topic is too narrow, it is difficult to find resources to support the thesis question. Similarly, the goal must be written to the scale of the embedded librarian project—not too broad or too narrow.

Realistic Goals

Realistic goals are those within your reach that are relevant to the librarian experiences, knowledge, and skills. These types of goals are consistent with past librarian work and library services, fitting well within the budget of the library and the workload of the librarian. The embedded librarian may need to discuss goals thoroughly with library administration to maintain the proper perspective in offering new services and the scale of the embedded project.

Setting realistic goals involves writing them down and referring to them regularly. Decide what is reasonable by determining the level of expertise currently attained and how the embedded project will affect workload. It is important not to over-promise as the failure of the delivery of embedded librarian services may affect credibility and future partnerships. Goals may need to be adjusted continually in the early stages of the partnership to be realistic and attainable.

Time-Based Goals

Creating a timeline for each goal will help with meeting commitments and later evaluating the embedded program. Goals must have a clearly defined starting and ending date. The time frame may be flexible, but there must be a method for marking the delivery dates for attaining each goal. The time-based goals built into the program will also mark major milestones within the project and provide a way to communicate progress and completion.

As the time frame is assembled within the goals, a logical sequence of steps will also emerge. Setting SMART goals step by step, ordered by priority or into smaller tasks that are easy to accomplish, will build new trust between the librarian and embedded partners. A new consistency will be established, and the librarian's reliability will increase as goals are accomplished on time. Meeting milestones will also assist with plan sustainability.

⊚ Checking Goals for Sustainability

Sustainability within the action plan is related to time frames and workload. The embedded librarian must work smart, identifying timeline problems or those that create larger workloads. As the embedded librarian begins fact-finding, selects embedded partners, and sets goals to work toward an embedded program, these goals must be examined practically to see how well they will lead to embedding the librarian within the outside organization. It may be necessary to chunk goals into smaller steps to meet timelines, but the objective should include full integration within the embedded group long term.

Before considering the creation of an embedded program, the librarian may have worked closely with academic departments, for example, who regularly request instruction sessions from library services. The librarian may want to increase the number of sessions, which focuses on transactions. A more sustainable goal would be developing new relationships within that academic department to learn more about problems students are encountering as they complete research assignments. Rather than waiting for faculty to request instruction, the librarian may go to them (virtually or physically) to discuss new approaches to the research assignment. The more sustainable goal would be to pursue working together on designing assignments and instruction that better addresses how to overcome fail points experienced during the assignment.

⊚ Constructing a Sustainable Action Plan

The sustainability of both the goals, their time frame, and the embedded librarian program must be a part of planning. New partnerships and relationships require trust and reliability. The embedded librarian must be sure to sustain communication and outreach efforts. Maintaining change may be a challenge, requiring librarians to create clear objectives, activities, roles, and timelines. Plans and the timelines may need to be adapted and changed as the embedded program is developed. A widely used definition for sustainable development is from the Brundtland Commission report *Our Common Future*: "development that meets the needs of the present without compromising the ability of future generations to meet their own needs" (1987: 43).

An action plan that only one individual could accomplish, where the success depends on a specific skill outside the normal job description for the librarian position, is not a sustainable plan. Goals that take up the entirety of the librarian's time are also not sustainable, as more staff may be needed to take over duties. Another consideration is the risk involved—does the goal adversely affect the library's goodwill within the community if the outcome is not accomplished? Any action plan has a potential for failure, and the risk management of a failed goal should be discussed within the goal-setting process. A backup plan or plan B may be considered if the goals have risky consequences. It is also important to involve all library staff who will be affected by the new embedded librarian program. Successful programs often create an increase in library usage—is the library prepared to serve such an increase?

Creating SMART goals, using both the earlier SWOT analyses to plan strategically and anticipating risk and reward, will help set up an effective action plan. Writing the action plan is a step that cannot be skipped as it will launch the embedded librarian into forging new collaborations, leading to embedded programs. Once the steps for goals creation have been identified, discussion with library administration, stakeholders, and librarians is needed to identify specific goals and determine how the planning will proceed. A sample action plan is also available in table 6.1.

Identifying Tools for Tracking and Communicating Progress

A new embedded librarian program will create the need for adjustments to schedules, communication, and availability of library staff and administration. Even if the program involves a virtually embedded librarian, changes in time spent on regular duties may change. An effective plan of action must include ways for the librarian to communicate what is being done and why. Roberts and Wood (2012) document five characteristics of operative strategic planning for libraries: aligning the plan to the vision of the library, providing clear direction, including stretch goals, bringing people together to work on a common goal, and strengthening the library brand. The action plan must be designed for maximizing library visibility while creating integrated partner programs to serve a shared mission. This shared mission should help drive the plan so that it is effective and based in the present reality, matching both the library and the embedded organization's goals, roles, and values. The result will be an action plan that will be used to communicate a shared sense of purpose and a natural alignment of the two institutions. It should be written to clearly convey an intent to serve the embedded community by exhibiting how the librarian will be of assistance to this group. The plan itself may be a useful communication device, and key strategies will include the communication of goals, purpose, and a timeline or tracking system.

An action plan that shares goal tracking systematically builds in an important level of communication and buy-in from the rest of the library staff. Frequent reports and working together toward supporting the embedded program is a positive team-building experience that may bring greater program success than anticipated. Most active embedded librarians have a strong services team at the library to support both librarian and organizational goals. Transparent communication about updates and progress made within the program help create synergy and excitement at the library. There are various tools available to create more visible tracking and to leverage communication opportunities within a good action plan. Here are the elements that are needed within these tools that will be the most helpful for an embedded librarian program:

- Tools with sharing components
- Sharing components with viewing, comments only, or editing options
- Tools that are accessible from any device with interoperability between devices
- Web-based or cloud-hosted tools

Action plans may range from printed templates with timelines to digital tools such as Google applications or LibGuides—internal or external to the community. The initial planning and goals should be written with detailed descriptions, but the resulting action plan may be more visual in nature. Infographics, graphs, or other visually represented action plan components may be easier to share, but will be dependent on the individual skills and abilities of the creator. There are many templates freely available online that use Microsoft Excel or Word and many others that have accompanying mobile apps. Tracking and communication may include both print and digital tools, such as shared calendars or monthly reports. Ease of use and clearly understandable communication are very important to staff who may be called upon to support new initiatives or services that result from new partnerships.

Many educational institutions and their librarians regularly use Google Apps due to the easy sharing and accessibility capabilities of these tools. Other libraries may use LibGuides or other free web tools such as a wiki or WordPress to share projects across locations or departments. When the action plan is initially created, a good discussion of which tools best work for tracking and communicating is as important as the actual plan. Although use of these tools may be new for library staff, the applicability of these tools to more library projects is well worth the training time. Also, learning about how to use these tools and how they will be used within the embedded librarian's work will create more staff ownership of the embedded librarian program.

The following goal-setting worksheet contains example tools that may be used to create an action plan by using the tips listed. This worksheet was created as a guide to include the elements discussed in this chapter.

GOAL-SETTING WORKSHEET

1. Interview partners using neutral questioning techniques and develop some ideas about challenges, initiatives, or changes where an embedded librarian opportunity may arise.
2. Write a detailed report that describes the challenges or goals of the organization the librarian hopes to embed with any timelines or deadlines included in the description.
3. Discuss the scenario with library administration or stakeholders (especially if in a solo librarian role) and discuss various ways library services or resources may be used to assist the organization.
4. Present the scenario to the rest of the staff and share possible goals and action items that are being discussed. Brainstorm new ideas and approaches with the staff and discuss time frames as well as who will participate from both the library and the organization.
5. Prioritize goals according to visibility, time, and impact factors.
6. Assign timelines and participants to each goal. Chunk complex goals into smaller steps.
7. Set up sharing, tracking, and communication tools. Provide training to staff as needed.
8. Work the action items and adhere to the timeline as you are able.
9. Provide regular reports to library administration, stakeholders, and staff.
10. Publicize successes no matter how small.

Whether a table, spreadsheet, or Google sheets are used to outline the action plan, the result must be viewable and shareable by library staff and administration. After the plan is outlined and shared, it is highly advisable to get input from other librarians and staff before finalizing the plan. Adding these perspectives from both frontline and administrative staff is especially helpful in setting the baseline of teamwork for the embedded librarian's actions. A brainstorming session, discussing alternative approaches or adding new services, is useful. It is also smart to build extra time into outlining to give staff reflection time for thinking about additional ideas. Participants in the action items may be identified as library staff; while they may not be held responsible for the final outcomes of the embedded program, they may play important roles in implementing services or creating new resources or services. The librarian should have a follow-up interview with the embedded partner to address added concerns or share ideas before finalizing the goals and timeline. These partners may already be using a goal-setting tool that may be adopted by the library for use in the program. Or the library may choose a completely different way to track and communicate progress within the embedded program.

Training may be needed for both library staff and embedded partners to keep everyone in the loop and make sure everyone understands how to use any new technology tools. The time frame for the action plan should include a training goal and actionable items to assess for understanding. Training must be followed up with application and tools usage on a regular basis to implement changes in communication among staff or partners. It is also possible that the librarian may need to operate using two different communication tools, one from the library and one from the embedded organization, to accomplish shared goals.

At this point, the librarian should create a new grid, outlining and setting up all the goals related to the embedded librarian project. Components in the spreadsheet of goals will include:

- Goals listed in priority order
- A list of action items in chronological order under each goal

Each action item should include the timeline for the item; a process owner for each item and a list of library staff participants (if applicable); a list of the embedded organization's participants in the action item; and a notes section to provide more information as time passes, which may help with the completion of the action item. A line (or column, depending on how you set up your grid) for staff ideas and comments is also important to include for each action item. List the library services or resources that will be used for each action item. If acquisitions are needed for new resources, the action item should outline how these will be acquired, including budgetary information and purchasing responsibilities. The timeline should also be used on either a print or digital shared calendar so that action items may be tracked by all participants and adjusted as needed. One more line, which includes a list of desired outcomes, will help all participants visualize the final product for the embedded project.

If the embedded librarian program involves only one of several librarians working at the library, the goals should also include a "train the trainer" opportunity to encourage other librarians to develop embedded programs in the future. Training may include team-teaching library instruction sessions, team interviews with embedded organization participants, and many other possibilities. The embedded program development affects the entire library, and it is important to collaborate with colleagues during the process and share ideas.

Table 6.1. Action Items for Embedding a Nursing Curriculum and Instruction Committee

EMBEDDED LIBRARIAN (BETTY THOMAS), NEW PROGRAM: MASTER OF SCIENCE, NURSING	
ACTION ITEM	**JOIN CURRICULUM AND INSTRUCTION COMMITTEE**
Process Owners	Betty Thomas, librarian; Jane Wui, NURS department chair; Jennifer Jordan, NURS MSN program director; Gena Garrett, library director
Library Staff Participants	Jeff Steel and Tom Smith, library tutorial designers; Jean Garcia, embedded librarian in BSN program
NURS Department Participants	Other members of NURS Curriculum and Instruction Committee from NURS department, Dean of NURS department
Notes	Committee will meet first Tuesdays at 2pm in room 106 Awaiting approval from Dean Bhatt
Library Resources	CINAHL Complete Access Medicine Micromedex
Acquisitions Needed	May need an additional nursing database—budget may allow $3,500 database expenditure
Timeline	Add librarian to committee by October meeting
Outcomes	Embedding librarian into curriculum design from the beginning Identifying courses with research component

⊚ Creating Time and Managing the Workload within the Action Plan

Creating time within a regular schedule to take all the steps needed to implement an action plan is complicated. Time and workload management needs should be discussed with the librarian's supervisor, colleagues, and possibly library stakeholders. These topics also should be discussed within the embedded organization with the embedded librarian and the new partners. Once the scope of the embedded project is identified, a final evaluation of this scope must be carefully considered to ensure its success. It may be necessary to scale down the project so that the librarian or the embedded partner can accomplish regular duties in addition to new embedded duties. Colleagues may be enlisted to temporarily ease workload, which can cause problems or affect the workloads of other library staff. It is important that the embedded project is not a burden to other library staff, possibly causing resentment or negativity toward the new program. The scope, the depth of the information gathered, and follow-up interviews must be clearly defined to move forward with planning.

Besides identifying the embedded project's scope, it is also important to plan carefully a logical order of action items. Keep the items simple and break down complex items into smaller steps. As steps progress within action items, barriers may arise. The embedded librarian may need to take time to gather more in-depth information to proceed. For this reason, it is important to space timelines so that there is breathing room and time to take extra steps as needed in gathering data or creating additional action items.

As shown throughout this chapter, communication and accountability are important in creating an effective action plan. The action plan requires a shared vision between the partnering organization, the librarian, and the library team. If the plan has high visibility for both parties and is mutually beneficial, a shared momentum will help bring all the goals within the plan to fruition. In addition, encouraging library staff, administrators, and stakeholders to view themselves as contributors to a team embedded librarian program results in strong support for the embedded librarian as well as the partnering organization.

Key Points

This chapter discusses how the librarian may prepare goals for implementing an action plan within an embedded program. Outcomes and objectives are outlined by simple steps to create a manageable and sustainable plan. These steps include and emphasize the following points:

- Thorough fact-finding strategies will help the librarian choose the best community candidates for an embedded librarian program.
- Setting SMART goals will help the embedded librarian take a logical approach to discussing the benefits of embedded programs to potential partners.
- Checking goals for sustainability during the planning stages will result in strong embedded programs that are integrated within the heart of the outside group.
- Constructing an action plan that is sustainable will help the librarian embed the group without reducing workload or library services provided beyond the embedded program.
- Identifying and using tools for tracking and communicating deliverables requires careful planning and staff training so that library staff may provide support to the embedded librarian program from its inception. The librarian must manage time and workload to open up a space for the creation of the embedded librarian partnership.

The next chapter will discuss creating a collaborative action plan with the embedded organization and developing partnerships and will provide tips for making these goals into a successful reality.

References

Barrett, Laura, and Katie Harding. 2017. "Librarians Are in the House! Unconventional Strategies for Outreach to Your Campus Community." ACRL 2017 Conference, 423–27. http://www .ala.org/acrl/sites/ala.org.acrl/files/content/conferences/confsandpreconfs/2017/Librarians AreintheHouse.pdf.

Brundtland Commission. 1987. *Our Common Future*. United Nations General Assembly, World Commission on Environment and Development. http://www.un-documents.net/ our-common-future.pdf.

Dervin, Brenda, and Patricia Dewdney. 1986. "Neutral Questioning: A New Approach to the Reference Interview." *Research Quarterly* 25, no. 4: 506–13. https://www.jstor.org/stable/25827718.

Doran, George T. 1981. "There's a S.M.A.R.T. Way to Write Management's Goals and Objectives." *Management Review* 70, no. 11: 35. *Business Source Complete*, EBSCO*host*.

Lyon, Jennifer A., Gretchen M. Kuntz, Mary E. Edwards, Linda C. Butson, and Beth Auten. 2015. "The Lived Experience and Training Needs of Librarians Serving at the Clinical Point-of-Care." *Medical Reference Services Quarterly* 34, no. 3 (July–September): 311–33. https://doi .org/10.1080/02763689.2015.1052693.

Maybee, Clarence, Tomalee Down, and Catherine Fraser Riehle. 2013. "Making an IMPACT: Campus-Wide Collaboration for Course and Learning Space Transformation." *Libraries Faculty and Staff Scholarship and Research*. Paper 15. https://doi.org/10.5860/crln.74.1.8884.

Roberts, Ken, and Daphne Wood. 2012. "Strategic Planning: A Valuable, Productive and Engaging Experience (Honest)." *Feliciter* 58, no. 5: 10–11. *Academic Search Complete*, EBSCO*host*.

Shumaker, David, and Alison Makins. 2012. "Lessons from Successful Embedded Librarians." *Information Outlook* 16, no. 3: 10–12. https://www.sla.org/wp-content/uploads/2013/05/ Lessons_from_Successful.pdf.

Stellrecht, Elizabeth, and Deborah Chiarella. 2015. "Targeted Evolution of Embedded Librarian Services: Providing Mobile Reference and Instruction Services Using iPads." *Medical Reference Services Quarterly* 34, no. 4 (October–December): 397–406. https://doi.org/10.1080/027 63869.2015.1082372.

St. Paul Public Library. 2017. "Resources on Race: Videos." Accessed September 10, 2017. http:// guides.sppl.org/resources-on-race/videos.

Urban Libraries Council. 2016. "Saint Paul Public Library Racial Equity Initiative, MN." *2016 Innovations: Urban Libraries Council.* https://www.urbanlibraries.org/saint-paul-public-library -racial-equity-initiative-innovation-1335.php?page_id=536.

Wu, Lin, and Misa Mi. 2013. "Sustaining Librarian Vitality: Embedded Librarianship Model for Health Sciences Libraries." *Medical Reference Quarterly* 32, no. 3 (July–September): 261–62. https://doi.org/10.1080/02763869.2013.806860.

Further Reading

Kenney, Anne R. 2014. "Leveraging the Liaison Model: From Defining 21st Century Research Libraries to Implementing 21st Century Research Universities." *Ithaka S+R.* https://doi .org/10.1865/sr.24807.

Kvenild, Cass. 2012. "The Future of Embedded Librarianship: Best Practices and Opportunities." *Proceedings of the California Conference on Library Instruction.* http://www.cclibinstruction.org/ wp-content/uploads/2012/02/CCLI2012proceedings_Kvenild.pdf.

Ndlovu, Sheila N. 2017. "Embedded Librarianship: The Key to Unlocking the Research Potential at Lupane State University." *Proceedings of the IATUL Conferences, Paper 2.* http://docs.lib .purdue.edu/iatul/2017/research/1.

Neubert, Mitchell J., and Bruno Dyck. 2016. "Developing Sustainable Management Theory: Goal-Setting Theory Based in Virtue." *Management Decision* 54, no. 2: 304–20. https://doi .org/10.1108/MD-05-2014-0312.

CHAPTER 7

Collaborative Action Planning for Embedded Librarianship

STARTING A NEW PLAN OF ACTION for embedded librarianship requires a leap of faith for most librarians. There are great rewards for personal satisfaction in forging new and collaborative relationships, but there also are possible ways to run into obstacles of your own creation. A collaborative action plan will serve as a road map to help accomplish objectives and navigate anticipated problems. The SWOT analysis described in chapter 3 will also be used as a reference tool for strategically planning the new venture into embedded librarianship.

Setting goals and creating a vision statement is an important first step. What do the librarian, the department that will be embedded, and administration hope to accomplish by venturing into embeddedness? As the plan is created, both for the librarian and for library stakeholders, objectives and resources must be in sync and a timeline must be included in the process. Visualization of the outcomes is important as well. Is this idea entirely new to the organization or an improved/expanded version of services already in place? Does the current library budget support the library plan to add more librarian services and possible time off the reference desk or other duties? Preliminary planning will help navigate issues such as staffing, budget, and timing. What intentions and aspirations are included within your planning? Have these plans been verbalized in a formal statement? "Verbalization is one of the most critical elements of the human behavioral repertoire, and can be used as a vehicle for organizing, directing, and evaluating action toward a goal" (Wang, 1996: 119). Collaborating with embedded partners to create shared goals may include outlining, creating formal plans, and verbalizing intentions from all involved.

A well-written plan is logical, concise, easy to understand, honest, and supported by research and documentation. Cohesiveness and careful attention to details and ordering the steps will help match talents to opportunities. A logical action plan will map future steps, communicate ideas to others, and serve as an operating tool that will help manage the embedded venture. Goals must be specific. The librarian will need to plan for changes in library resources or services and try to envision what will be different or more beneficial for the organization the librarian plans to embed.

The librarian may not have expertise in strategic planning or project management, but writing down the action plan is a step that cannot be skipped. This chapter outlines the working components or nuts and bolts of planning. Five elements are vital to constructing the plan:

- Research
- Planning
- Setting goals
- Establishing relationships
- Evaluation

⑥ Researching the Embedded Program's Information Needs

Researching the group that a librarian plans to embed is a necessary part of creating a plan. This research may be compared to the type of research needed for collection development or redesigning a website. Building a useful library collection depends on the librarian's understanding of the needs of the library community. For example, if a library contemplates purchasing a new database, the database usually is offered on a trial basis to the community. During the trial period the library may add a link to the web page and ask for feedback. The trial period helps the library determine if the new database is going to be of use to its patrons, and most librarians work to market the trial and discuss, especially with its library champions, whether this new addition to the collection is wanted or needed. Likewise, when a library redesigns its website, it often provides a link to the beta site to get feedback and fix problems in advance of premiering the new website. Usability of materials or the website in both situations is very important to test and acquire input in moving forward. Although the reader has already completed a SWOT analysis in a previous chapter and analyzed ideas and ways the librarian may embed the outside group, research is still needed to determine the most useful and mutually beneficial way to proceed for all concerned. He or she may have some ideas of where the presence of an embedded librarian may have an impact on the outside group, but these ideas are merely assumptions at this point. The librarian needs to talk to various members of this outside group, ideally someone who already uses the library on a regular basis, to get feedback about ideas for embedding the group. During the SWOT analysis, various opportunities are identified and the librarian needs to start a conversation, similar to a reference interview, in order to determine the first step for the action plan. Another way to initiate contact is to poll or survey group members to open the discussion about opportunities the librarian may have observed.

Interviews

The embedded librarian will need to determine the needs of the new partnering department or organization, and using the same techniques used for reference interviews will help move the process forward. Closed questions, which may be answered with yes or no, may be combined with open-ended questions—those that elicit more details and neutral questions—asking for more clarification as a subset of open questions. An article by Dervin and Dewdney (1986) describes how to approach an interview using these two types of questions, open ended and close ended. Neutral questioning avoids premature problem solving and centers the questions around the information needs of the interviewed participants. Techniques in this article help save time in interviewing the potential embedded partner as it easily uncovers needs, goals, and aspirations that the librarian may choose to address within the scope of the embedded project. The librarian will need to see issues to be addressed using the embedded partner perspective rather than guessing these needs. Dervin developed the term "neutral questioning" in 1981 to describe communication strategies to enable "the librarian to understand the query from the user's point of view" by asking about "specific elements—situations, gaps, uses" (Dervin and Dewdney, 1986: 508, 510). Sample questions may be used to address these three elements as follows:

- Situations
  - You say you are now requiring student groups to present posters as a part of their grade. How are you working toward this goal?
  - It sounds like you are not happy with the quality of sources your students are using in their research. Tell me more about this issue.
  - Concern about fake news is a popular topic with other English professors as well. How are you addressing this issue within your course?
  - How are you getting contact information out to the community about disaster assistance?
  - As you present children's programs at the library, do you think about developing programming for parents?
  - During health fairs it is very common to get in-depth consumer health questions. What types of questions have you been asked and how did you handle the situation?

- Gaps
  - What would you like to know about organizing a poster competition for your department?
  - What do you want your students to understand about evaluating the information they find for their research papers?
  - What is missing as you try to educate students about how to evaluate media sources?
  - How does the high school promote reading without a school librarian?
  - I noticed your information booth during your Breast Cancer Walk last weekend. What kinds of questions do you get at that event?

- Uses

  - How do group poster presentations benefit your students?
  - If you could have help in evaluating information, what kind of assistance would be the most useful to you and your students?
  - What outcomes are you expecting so that you know students now understand how to identify fake news?
  - How do you easily find answers to the consumer health questions asked at these events?
  - What types of sources do you post on your website to answer questions from the public?
  - What resources do your employees go to first to find out benchmarking information?

SAMPLE SCRIPT FOR PUBLIC LIBRARIAN WANTING TO EMBED THE LOCAL MARCH OF DIMES ANNUAL WALK

This sample script may be used as a conversation starter for a public librarian who wants to embed services into a community activity.

Librarian: We usually post flyers about your Annual March of Dimes Walk at our library. Several staff members also walk and collect donations each year. We've also noticed that many patrons, especially following the March of Dimes Walk, come to the library to find information about birth defects and get help from our librarians to research these conditions. There is so much health information available online—have you found that people have trouble locating information they need from a source that can be trusted?

March of Dimes Walk director: Thanks for posting our flyers and participating in the walk. People do tell us they have trouble finding information about birth defects as well.

Librarian: We have a lot of information here at our library about finding good sources for all kinds of health questions, including birth defects. We have been talking about partnering with your group this year, not only to promote your walk, but also to help the participants learn more about their health. Would you be interested?

A quality reference interview is not a "marketing the library" promotional type of presentation. The librarian must discover along with the user what information is actually needed and the scope of that need. Great interview techniques for a thorough reference interview include paraphrasing ("So I understand you are saying you need X"), asking open-ended questions ("Could you tell me more about it?"), and clarifying the information needs for the patron. As in the reference interview, the librarian needs to verify how an embedded librarian may be needed in the outside group by asking questions and sharing ideas about new ways the embedded model of assistance may be helpful to the group. Even frequent users at the library may not be aware of services the library provides or even how a librarian may be of help to their group.

SAMPLE SCRIPT FOR A LIBRARIAN AT A COMMUNITY COLLEGE TALKING TO AN ENGLISH PROFESSOR ABOUT INFORMATION LITERACY SESSIONS FOR ENG 1301

This example may be used by a librarian who is either trying to initiate a conversation with a professor or accidentally runs into a professor at the library.

Librarian: I really enjoy teaching the one-shot information literacy classes for your students each semester. I have noticed your students come for help after class at the library reference desk, which is great, but many of them have stated that the class has too much information and it can be overwhelming. Many of them have selected topics that are too broad or too narrow, and they have trouble finding the information needed to support these topics. I have been working on a different model of instruction to supplement the IL classes, to address student needs step by step as they write their essays.

Professor: Yes, the topics seem to be a real problem for them. Last semester during your class you showed the students a brief "Choosing a Topic" tutorial on the library website. I found myself wishing I had known about this resource beforehand so that I could direct my students to go through the tutorial before choosing a topic.

Librarian: We librarians are always adding new tutorials and LibGuides to help the students, but we are aware that we have trouble getting the information out to faculty and students.

Professor: This problem seems to be ongoing. . . . You mentioned a different model for information literacy instruction—could you tell me more about it?

The approach used at the reference desk works well in researching how best to serve and embed an organization. A welcoming, interested but neutral demeanor is important in uncovering gaps or information needs. Active listening skills such as repeating back what was articulated to confirm understanding are just as useful in outreach as at the reference desk. The key is to learn how best to assist with librarian expertise and knowledge without confusing issues with library jargon. Consistency in approach and following up builds trust and an expectation of reliability. First discussions with new partnerships work best if simplified language rather than typical library terminology is used. Buzzwords commonly used among librarians such as information literacy or UX (user experience) will need to be defined within the context of the embedded organization. It is equally important to have a full understanding of all the library resources and services available so as to address information needs within an appropriate parameter. The embedded librarian will be able to assist with all observed information needs with a solid understanding of what may be provided.

> ## SAMPLE SCRIPT FOR A MEDICAL LIBRARIAN MEETING
> ## WITH A PHARMACY FACULTY AT A UNIVERSITY
> ## TO PROPOSE EMBEDDING IN THE DEPARTMENT
>
> This script gives an example of a health sciences librarian who wishes to discuss an embedded librarian role at the end of a faculty meeting.
>
> *Librarian*: I wanted to bounce off some ideas with you to better help the faculty teaching drug literature courses as well as those who prepare students for their clinical rounds during their final year in pharmacy school. I really enjoy teaching your classes how to research, but I have noticed many of the faculty within your department struggle to use the library for research. For example, many have trouble finding full text for articles and get very frustrated.
>
> *Pharmacy professor*: Well, you know, things have changed a lot since I got my degree. Everything is online, and I find your website somewhat complicated to use.
>
> *Librarian*: I was thinking about creating a brief presentation for faculty to be used at your departmental meetings this year to help faculty research more effectively. I thought I could structure it to answer one frequently asked question per month, such as "How do I find full-text articles found in the PubMed database?" or "What pharmacy or drug databases does the library have available for clinical rounds?" Does this sound like a useful idea for the department?
>
> *Pharmacy professor*: That is a good idea—I know all of us have trouble keeping current with the literature in our field.

Surveys

If the librarian does not have access to many group members of the embedded department available to meet with or to interview, a survey may be another way to begin to research the information needs of the outside group. Numerous free polling software programs are available for this purpose, including SurveyMonkey or Doodle poll. The questions may be directed toward making the participants aware of new resources such as materials, databases, LibGuides, or services. Questions geared toward a Likert scale or open-ended questions will usually help identify sources or embedded librarian services needed by the group. For example, the questions may include information about information literacy sessions, tutorials, or new materials. If a poll or survey is used, it should be followed up with an individual interview with the participants.

Survey design will not be covered comprehensively in this book, but there are many sources available for this purpose. Here are a few great sources to learn more about creating well-designed surveys:

- Fink, Arlene G. 2017. *How to Conduct Surveys: A Step-by-Step Guide*. 6th ed. Thousand Oaks, CA: Sage.
- Fowler, Floyd J., Jr. 2014. *Survey Research Methods*. 5th ed. Thousand Oaks, CA: Sage.
- Pew Research Center. 2018. *U.S. Survey Research: Questionnaire Design*. http://www.pewresearch.org/methodology/u-s-survey-research/questionnaire-design/.

The librarian may also consider a pre-survey and/or post-survey for learning about user perceptions of the embedded librarian services. There are several example surveys available in the literature, such as the post-survey by Blake et al. (2016) at a health sciences academic library, which included questions about the effectiveness of a new embedded librarian program. Questions like these may be adapted for use as a pre-survey to determine expectations, needs, gaps, and services that may be targeted in action planning. Surveys may also be used to lay the groundwork for learning and collaboration. Participants may use survey results to reflect upon and develop learning communities to engage students in improved information literacy practices. Academic library surveys to both students and faculty may uncover insights into research proficiencies and writing experiences and can begin to open conversations about the research process.

Survey results about undergraduate research practices are available as additional tools for discussing embedded academic librarian needs from Project Information Literacy (PIL). Alison Head presented PIL's most recent summative report at ACRL 2013, which examined gaps in information literacy competencies for undergrads. The report lists major setbacks students encounter while trying to complete a research assignment. More than eleven thousand U.S. college students were surveyed about their information-seeking behavior and search strategies for issues within their daily lives. Survey results included the difficulties encountered in finding good sources and developing a well-defined topic to search (Head, 2013). These issues make excellent discussion points to consider for inclusion into the action plan and may be used as interview topics as well as suggested survey questions.

Following are some ideas for short survey questions:

- What information competencies matter at the workplace within your discipline?
- How do your students find and process information for their assignments?
- How do your employees research how other companies accomplish similar goals?
- What library resources are you most familiar with?
- What difficulties do new faculty experience in performing research within their field?
- How does your organization resolve information problems?

Communication

One of the most important parts for this research step includes identifying how best to communicate with the outside group. Communication problems will exist within any organization, but most will have a preferred form of communication that generally works well for everyone. It is important to research how members of the group convey information and identify what is most effective for future use. Learning how the new group expects to receive communication will affect the embedded librarian's daily routine. For example, faculty may be required to answer emails from a departmental Listserv or from students within a twenty-four-hour period. Other groups may get so much email from students that they depend on the learning management software to keep student emails all in one place. Some workplaces depend heavily on the phone for important conversations, while other companies may not provide each employee an individual phone extension.

Researching the method of communication is a good beginning, but it is also important to investigate the culture of communication. How does the department communicate, and who needs to be included in the conversation? What steps need to be taken to move forward on a project? Understanding the organizational culture will play a major role in the success of the embedded librarian. Organizational culture includes how the people within the group behave and why they behave that way, based on cultural norms and values. "Cultures are dynamic. They shift, incrementally and constantly, in response to external and internal changes" (Watkins, 2013). The librarian will need to ask questions to make sense of the newly embedded group.

If the librarian does not have clearly identified ideas for becoming an embedded part of the outside group, it may be useful to also interview outside group members about how to best improve communications and the relationships between the library, librarians, and the new group. The librarian may want to define embedded librarianship for the group and discuss ideas for embedding the group. These ideas will include in-depth knowledge of information literacy skills and methods for integration. Group discussions will help develop a sense of the values of the new partners and new organizational intelligence. The librarian must be prepared with examples of new services or fulfilling needs observed as he or she wrote in the SWOT analysis. After completing the interview process and this research step, the librarian should have some concrete ideas of where to best serve the group.

Planning Shared Outcomes with Collaborative Partners

Most individuals have experience in setting goals as well as making a plan that states how those goals will be realized. Establishing goals is an important project and time management tool that traditionally leads to success. For example, a student decides to complete courses needed to acquire a bachelor's degree in a chosen field. Traditional goal planning is vital for good results. As the librarian begins to work with new partners to establish an embedded librarian program, goal setting takes on a new dimension. A shared value system will develop within this new partnership. Desired outcomes for both the librarian and embedded partner's efforts will be included in the process. There are several methods that may be used to create shared outcomes. These include using backward design and structuring the program using tracking tools for continued growth or sustainability.

Backward Design

An innovative approach to creating an action plan includes applying principles of backward design. Backward design is a valuable method to use in constructing goals and objectives for the embedded librarian action plan. This type of design process examines desired outcomes and designs goals and objectives that will produce these outcomes. It is an important tool to use in both curriculum design and project management. The process begins with visualizing the end result and identifying what means will be used to realize the desired result. For example, the outcome may be the establishment of a K–6 information literacy curriculum within an elementary school. Another outcome may be integrating the librarian as a member of the pediatric surgical team within the clinical faculty at a hospital. This methodology is also helpful in the success of the action plan, as the librarian must visualize him- or herself as a part of the plan's desired results. Visualization is a very positive tool in attaining complicated goals. "Consider the root causes of present achievement, and then—and only then—implement systematic actions to address root causes" (McTighe and Thomas, 2003: 55).

A shared vision of successful outcomes is invaluable to this stage of planning. The embedded partners must determine together what criteria will be used to define a successful result. What will an effective embedded program look like? After shared outcomes have been identified, the librarian must think carefully about the steps and processes needed to arrive at the outcome. A results-driven plan rather than a content-focused plan will keep the emphasis on how an embedded librarian will impact the other organization. Wiggins and McTighe (2005) created easily understandable stages of backward design: "identify desired results, determine acceptable evidence, and plan learning experiences and instruction." Desired results of an embedded librarian program include demonstrating knowledge of new information literacy concepts, new information-seeking behaviors, and their application within the embedded environment. For an embedded academic department, this new information may be demonstrated by both faculty and students.

Backward planning is also beneficial within this stage of the process as a timeline will slowly be created as the librarian plans the implementation of the plan objectives within the embedded program. As the action plan begins to materialize, it will not look very different on paper from a traditional plan, where the goals are written, followed by the steps needed to achieve the goals; the objectives and outcomes are written last. The difference in using backward design is the element of imagining what appearance the outcome will assume. By starting at the end and planning backward, the planning process will include the element of a well-defined successful outcome. The librarian will write down in the action plan—what will be the plan's impact—before planning the steps to make the impact. The outcome will indicate transformational change and perhaps organization change as well. This different perspective of planning the outcome rather than setting goals and hoping they will be accomplished is important in designing the plan. The backward design methodology will provide evidence that the change has taken place.

Table 7.1. Examples of Shared Outcomes in a First-Year Experience Class

LIBRARIAN OUTCOME	COURSE INSTRUCTOR OUTCOME	SHARED OUTCOME
Students will use library databases to find articles for their assignment on careers.	Students will use better sources in their research assignment.	Students will learn how to find credible sources for their research assignment.
Students will learn how to use the CRAAP test to evaluate information.	Students will learn how to recognize fake news.	Students will learn how to evaluate information.
Students will explore the concept that scholarship is a conversation.	Students will cite their sources using MLA style formatting.	Students will learn how to use information ethically and understand the role their research plays within the scholarship of a discipline.

Structuring the Plan with Tracking Tools

Important elements in creating the action plan include determining the scope of your embedded project. As planning commences, embedded partnerships set timelines and discuss tracking the shared timeline. Partners will want to determine what tools will be used to monitor the project's progress and budget. Additional tools may be used for planning growth, communication, and sustainability.

Sustainability, or the ability to continue working as an embedded librarian in the capacity identified within the project, is a major element. Working many hours outside of a regular workweek or assuming duties that only the embedded librarian can perform may set up the embedded relationships for failure.

There are many project management technology tools freely available to use in tracking the progress of the plan. These tools track time frames, deadlines, and milestones and assist in determining the best ways to achieve goals. As mentioned earlier, when the librarian initiates the research phase at the beginning of the project planning process, a communication plan will also materialize as the librarian learns more about how the group interacts. It is also important to learn how the outside organization tracks projects. Using the same tools is very helpful in embedding the group culture. Many organizations have preferred tech tools for document sharing and project management, such as sharing Google Docs or using Trello or Teamwork to manage projects. Using similar tools will improve the communication between the librarian and the group, and monitoring progress will help the librarian communicate with administrative groups at the library and the new organization.

Tracking tools may be used to set a baseline and provide visuals to see progress, growth, or continuing goals. New project management tools are developed each year, and it would date the material in this chapter to be too specific about recommended software. There are some components common to most software that work well for an embedded librarian program, such as checklists, color-coding, ways to see a summary of details and hover or click on the summary for full details, and time-stamping. Shared calendars are also useful for communication and transparency for all involved in the project. The embedded librarian will be able to schedule meetings using the shared calendar and easily find the best time to connect with embedded partners.

Setting Goals: Relating Goals to the SWOT Analysis

Backward design planning also helps anticipate obstacles or problem areas within the process used to arrive at the outcomes for the plan. Once the outcomes are determined and there is a good idea of what evidence will show these are being achieved, the goals and processes may be written and structured. Find ways to assess the progress toward the outcomes and write these into the plan as well. The goals should be simple and easy to measure and attain. Start by breaking up the goals into structured chunks with timelines and small steps. Utilize relationships already established to discuss goals and make them manageable and simple.

During the SWOT analysis, both the target group chosen for the embedded project and the library are examined (reminder—the SWOT analysis is described in chapter 3). Once the SWOT analysis is completed, divide the results of this analysis into suggested areas to embed and write goals and objectives related to each area. The movement from SWOT analysis, fact-finding, and research to creating shared goals may seem confusing. The embedded librarian and new partner will need to brainstorm ideas to resolve threats, maximize opportunities, or turn perceived weaknesses into strengths.

Following is an example relating a medical librarian's set of goals to the W part of the SWOT analysis (weaknesses) area. The librarian, who is embedded in the university pharmacy department, has identified a weakness within the program with pharmacy faculty partners. Students entering the clinical part of the degree program report difficulties in locating practice guidelines at point of care during rounds. A shared goal related to the SWOT analysis is created. The embedded partners agree that there is a knowledge gap, and the embedded librarian suggests meeting that information need using clinical library database mobile apps and a LibGuide with more clinical resources. The embedded librarian works together with the clinic coordinator to embed online instruction modules for locating clinical information easily at the point of need. A new fourth-year introductory module is created to help the students set up mobile library database tech tools and learn how to find basic clinical information. This example shows how shared goals may be created resulting from the SWOT analysis.

Another way to develop related goals is to describe the end product—what the result would look like, what role would be played by the librarian in this situation, what indicators would show the librarian is embedded, and who would be involved within the process. An example list of outcomes could be something like this one—an embedded librarian within a PhD education program would possibly be included as a guest lecturer in research/writing courses throughout the semester, have access to the courseware for each section, provide faculty professional development in understanding the changing dynamics of the publishing world, and regularly consult with PhD students on their writing projects. This list could be related to O—opportunities in the SWOT analysis—points of need identified for librarian intervention.

The goal developed from these opportunities may be to move from one-shot instruction sessions to course integration. For example, the embedded librarian may add these outcomes within an entire semester for a course that uses a capstone paper as part of the assessment for the course. Processes for arriving at the outcomes and achieving this goal may include regular consultations with education faculty and integrating tutorials/library resources into the syllabus for the course. Completion of steps needed for the capstone project may include grading activities related to information literacy assignments as well as traditional education assignments.

⊚ Establishing Trusting Relationships within the Embedded Organization

An action plan with substance requires planning for collaboration opportunities. Flexibility, cooperation, and teamwork are important for communication and achieving shared goals and objectives. Plan processes may need to be modified or adjusted due to circumstances beyond either the group's or librarian's control. For example, a key library resource used within the embedded project may be lost due to budget constraints or vendor changes. These threats to the success of the project may be addressed smoothly if the shared outcome is visualized and those involved are willing to try another method or work together to experiment with new ideas.

Building relationships with users is a natural role within librarianship. Every library has library champions, who make days brighter by their enthusiastic interactions while using the library. Some libraries can create sustaining partnerships with teachers, parents, community members, and outside organizations. These partnerships are built upon consistent policies, welcoming staff attitudes, and library resources that meet the informational needs of the users. Libraries plan for consistent policies and aim to communicate these policies clearly, creating good patron relationships. The embedded librarian will need to view relationships as a targeted outcome, rather than a by-product of other actions.

Establishing trustworthy partnerships should be listed as a shared goal, for all types of embedded librarian programs. Transitioning into an embedded partner relationship may be tricky, as it often requires a new level of political navigation and trust building. There are some strategic techniques that may help you cement and polish your new relationship within an embedded organization with your new partners.

Trust is an important element in any lasting relationship, and a commitment to building trust within the partnership is important. Embedded librarian programs are mutually beneficial partnerships as both sides of the partnership experience growth and a shared vision. Acknowledging that success is dependent on both partners is particularly important as goals are accomplished. An emphasis on working together as a great team, mutual respect, and an appreciation of what each partner brings to the table is important. As each action item takes the program forward, the librarian and library administration should reach out to the outside organization to recognize the efforts of the partners within the organization who helped meet the desired outcomes.

Open and honest communication as well as sharing fears and problems encountered will help the relationship to grow as well. Frequent discussions of shared goals are important as things may change; both partners need to keep the other apprised of any changes to adjust in planning and implementing new parts of the goals. Strive for maintaining a win-win situation and be careful to keep internal organizational communications confidential.

There are many resources available for fostering partnerships outside the library. The DIY blog (2015) has an excellent interactive tool for guiding new partners and mapping pathways to create better relationships with both potential and active partners. Once an embedded librarian program achieves a level of success and the partnership becomes more stable, the partners may want to discuss the sustainability of the embedded librarian program and whether to institutionalize the program. These are natural steps in any solid partnership and one of the hallmarks of a successfully embedded librarian.

Collaboration and teamwork must be included in the outcomes, goals, and objectives for the embedded librarian. An article in the 2009 journal *Education* states, "It should be noted that the intentionality . . . is nearly as important as the sequence itself" (Jones, Vermette, and Jones, 2009: 360). Building relationships with members of the embedded group is vital to reaching desired outcomes. A fully embedded team is the ideal big picture for the strategic plan. Creating trust and learning the best way to work, as a team happens slowly and naturally. Until the librarian is fully embedded, plan for taking careful notes and track conversations, deadlines, and when to check back with new partners. Detailed tracking will be very helpful in moving forward and keeping the embedded project aligned with objectives.

Table 7.2. Example of Non-collaborative vs. Collaborative Instruction

NON-COLLABORATIVE INSTRUCTION	COLLABORATIVE INSTRUCTION
Librarian has limited access to student instruction (one-shot session).	Librarian has multi-contact points for interacting with students throughout the semester.
Librarian examines syllabus and makes suggestions.	Instructor and librarian design curriculum and instructional delivery.
Instructor works with a different librarian each semester.	Instructor develops a working relationship with a single librarian or a small group of librarians.

There are several purposeful strategies that work well in embedded academic programs. One that works well for most librarians is mindful engagement in casual or formal deliberate talks with faculty. Approach conversations as reference interviews and advocate for mutual interests in information literacy or technology. Find ways to connect that make a difference for student success. Uncover information needs with the knowledge gained in these moments. Offer to make formal presentations at departmental or staff development meetings. Offer information not only about how librarians help students but also how they help faculty. School or public librarians may also want to pursue strategic conversations within the embedded organization. Volunteer to join committees and work together within the embedded organization. Work to develop a clear understanding of the political climate, and strive to remain neutral but interested as a member of the embedded group. Adjust your mind-set to view yourself as a true partner instead of wondering if they are questioning your participation in the embedded group. Each partner brings something unique to the relationship. Successful collaboration requires shared leadership and shared expectations of partner roles. Some partners work together better than others.

The degree to which the librarian is embedded within the program may vary depending on the willingness of the other party to collaborate. Patience along with strong evidence supporting the embedded librarian partnership will see the project through. Data collection and its analysis plays an important role in an embedded program's growth and sustainability.

◎ Evaluating and Managing Stages of the Embedded Action Plan

Evaluation and assessment for reaching objectives, clearly indicating evidence of the success of goals, is important for justifying time spent on any embedded librarian project. Each stage of the embedded action plan must be managed well. Successful embedded librarians spend many hours on these projects, and an indication of value attached to the result is important for continuing the program and budget planning. If the library does not have many librarians, careful evaluation of time spent versus outcomes met will be very important in assessing the success of the program.

The success of the project may also be indicated by outcomes that are not a part of the original plan. As new relationships are developed during the embedded processes, new opportunities may arise that were not anticipated within the planning stage. Collaborative efforts to manage shared goals within the action plan will help embedded partners learn how to work smarter and how to operate as an embedded team.

Evaluation plays an important role within the action plan as it helps the embedded librarian and the outside group establish stronger partnerships. Evaluation may have both shared and individual components, depending on how the data will be shared. This topic will be covered in more detail in the next chapter, but it is important to think about the role evaluation plays in managing shared goals. Various ideas for evaluation include the use of surveys, data analysis, self-evaluation, and shared observations.

Pre- and Post-survey Evaluations

It is common to survey students for feedback within the academic environment for instructor evaluations. An article on evaluating an embedded librarian pilot by Lin Wu and colleagues is recommended reading. This pilot at the University of Tennessee Health

Sciences nursing program addressed the quality of research writing within the MSN program. The embedded librarian role became a part of the course syllabus, with value-added services such as guest lectures, citation management tool training, and designing a course guide. Pre- and post-survey questions were loaded into the course management system. Students were also encouraged to self-evaluate their competency in finding authoritative health information (Wu et al., 2013). The surveys allowed both the course instructor and embedded librarian to gain a shared understanding of what embedded services were most useful to students. Additional data collected and used to evaluate the program was a record of student questions emailed to the embedded librarian. An increase in the number of questions as well as the type of questions asked is also useful data to observe the effectiveness of the embedded program.

The results of the survey helped the embedded partners develop improved course design, and they began to share more teaching duties. The librarian and course instructor were able to manage and adjust shared goals and outcomes to better serve the information needs of the students.

Data Analysis of Embedded Librarian Reference Questions

A similar study using an analysis of emailed reference questions was also undertaken by Kumar, Wu, and Reynolds in 2014. The University of Tennessee (UT) Health Sciences Library and the Department of Health Information and Information Management at the UT Health Science Center in Memphis examined the content of emailed questions from graduate students taking a research concepts course. The embedded librarian had a special "Embedded Librarian" area within Blackboard, and librarian content was included in the course syllabus. The evaluation for this program also used pre- and post-surveys, gaining valuable feedback, but the analysis of questions revealed the levels of interaction with the embedded librarian. Areas where students needed specialized assistance included the following:

- How to synthesize research and build a research paper
- How to review the literature on their topics
- How to choose a good topic

(Kumar, Wu, and Reynolds, 2014)

This mixed methodology of combining surveys and data analysis worked well for this institution. The results not only showed the impact of the librarian on the program, but also pointed to areas where students needed more instruction and resources for success. The embedded librarian collaborated with the instructor and academic department to build upon their knowledge for future embedded librarian projects.

Self-Evaluation: The Kirkpatrick Model

The Kirkpatrick model created by Dr. Don Kirkpatrick in the 1950s is a popular method for evaluating the effectiveness of formal or informal training. These four levels are evaluated:

- Reaction: how the learners react or engage with the training
- Learning: the amount of content/skills learned during the training

- Behavior: whether the behavior of the learners changes after the training
- Results: how well student learning outcomes are demonstrated or put into practice

(Mind Tools Content Team, 2017)

Kirkpatrick's model is especially effective for use in self-evaluation for the embedded librarian and finding areas for improvement as well as shared self-evaluations for both the librarian and embedded partners.

Self-evaluation for both the librarian and the embedded partners plays an important role in managing future collaborations. Sharing the results builds community and concretizes the action plan. Learning how to better work with each other improves future embedded endeavors.

Teaching Observations

One of the most valuable resources for evaluating the effectiveness of the embedded librarian is the use of observations and team teaching. The librarian and instructor working together to help students learn how to research and best practices for writing is a powerful combination. Trust and mutual respect can help build a strong partnership. Both the embedded librarian and the instructor need to work to develop ways to give each other input and improve student outcomes. Sharing what is working, talking through what is not working, and coming together to resolve obstacles to student understanding course content is vital to the partnership.

A recommended tool for establishing an evaluative framework for observations is Gagne's nine events of instruction. The nine events aid in lesson planning, active learning activities, and creating instructional topics for observation and subsequent instruction; they are as follows:

1. Gain the attention of the student.
2. Inform the learners of the learning objectives.
3. Stimulate recall of prior knowledge.
4. Present new content.
5. Provide learning guidance.
6. Ask for demonstration of knowledge.
7. Provide feedback for improvement.
8. Assess performance.
9. Enhance retention and application of knowledge.

(Woo, 2016)

Each of the numbered events may be addressed in observations and working together with the course instructor. It is important to know that no instructional session is perfect, and the nine events will not necessarily occur at each class session. The events are most useful when viewed as a framework for systematic learning and team teaching. It gives structure to conversations about how well the embedded program is working for faculty, students, and the librarian.

Successfully embedded librarians get started with small steps, approaching known library champions and discussing ideas for embedded projects before formalizing their plans. Using surveys, teaching observations, or other evaluation tools at the onset of the embedded librarian program helps both the librarian and embedded group experience small successes and learn how they may manage the action plan.

The path of least resistance is a great starting place. It is important to start small with evaluations and make first goals easily attainable to build confidence for all involved stakeholders. Manage the stages of the program systematically using self-evaluation tools as well as shared methodologies. Consider the roles already established with the embedded partners. Collaborations may already be in place, and creating an action plan that builds on earlier accomplishments is wise and usually works well. Transparency works well for communicating how well the partnership is developing and sharing small successes along the way.

Interview group members to look at the project from a different perspective and systematically chunk information literacy needs that relate to your SWOT analysis. Take both formal and informal opportunities such as formal meetings and informal casual conversations to build relationships with the targeted embedded group members. Look for chances to engage group members in talking about their aspirations and goals to learn more about their information needs. Actively join the group, but always maintain the embedded librarian identity.

Key Points

This chapter outlines collaborative action planning using research and shared planning. It is important to research carefully to lay the groundwork for support and buy-in from both the library and the embedded organization. Trust may be developed with relationship building and shared goals.

- Researching the embedded program's information needs helps in creating mutual goals shared by the librarian and the embedded organization.
- Planning shared outcomes involving collaborative partners builds community and embedded teamwork.
- Setting goals and relating goals to the SWOT analysis creates buy-in from the embedded group.
- Collaborating with and establishing trusting relationships within the embedded organization should be a shared goal within any embedded partnership plan.
- Evaluating and managing stages of the embedded action plan plays an important role in setting the tone for the embedded partnership by taking small steps, especially at the beginning of the embedded relationship.

Collaborative action planning is important, and flexibility built into the plan will help establish value and effectiveness of the embedded librarian program. The next chapter will discuss different methodologies for adjusting the action plan, customizing parameters, and evaluating the success of the embedded librarian.

References

Blake, Lindsay, Darra Ballance, Kathy Davies, Julie K. Gaines, Kim Mears, Peter Shipman, Maryska Connolly-Brown, and Vicki Burchfield. 2016. "Patron Perception and Utilization of an Embedded Librarian Program." *Journal of the Medical Library Association* 104, no. 3 (July): 226–30. https://doi.org/10.3163/1536-5050.104.3.008.

Dervin, Brenda, and Patricia Dewdney. 1986. "Neutral Questioning: A New Approach to the Reference Interview." *Research Quarterly* 25, no. 4: 506–13. https://www.jstor.org/stable/25827718.

DIY. 2015. "Building a Partnership Map." *Development Impact & You: Practical Tools to Trigger and Support Social Innovation* (blog). 2015. http://diytoolkit.org/tools/building-partnerships-map-2/.

Head, Alison J. 2013. "Project Information Literacy: What Can Be Learned about the Information-Seeking Behavior of Today's College Students?" ACRL Indianapolis, 2013. http://www.projectinfolit.org/uploads/2/7/5/4/27541717/head_project.pdf.

Jones, Karrie A., Paul J. Vermette, and Jennifer L. Jones. 2009. "An Integration of 'Backwards Planning' Unit Design with the 'Two-Step' Lesson Planning Framework." *Education* 130, no. 2: 357–60. *Academic Search Complete*, EBSCO*host*.

Kumar, Sajeesh, Lin Wu, and Rebecca Reynolds. 2014. "Embedded Librarian within an Online Health Informatics Graduate Research Course: A Case Study." *Medical Reference Services Quarterly* 33, no. 1: 51–59. https://doi.org/10.1080/02763869.2014.866485.

McTighe, Jay, and Ronald S. Thomas. 2003. "Backward Design for Forward Action." *Educational Leadership* 60, no. 5: 52–55. *Academic Search Complete*, EBSCO*host*.

Mind Tools Content Team. 2017. "Kirkpatrick's Four Level Training Evaluation Model: Analyzing Training Effectiveness." MindTools.com. https://www.mindtools.com/pages/article/kirkpatrick.htm.

Wang, Shouhong. 1996. "Toward Formalized Object-Oriented Management Information Systems Analysis." *Journal of Management Information Systems* 12, no. 4: 117–41. *Business Source Complete*, EBSCO*host*.

Watkins, Michael D. 2013. "What Is Organizational Culture? And Why Should We Care?" *Harvard Business Review*, May 15, 2013. https://hbr.org/2013/05/what-is-organizational-culture.

Wiggins, Grant, and Jay McTighe. 2005. *Understanding by Design*. Alexandria, VA: Association for Supervision and Curriculum Development. http://ecosensing.org/wp-content/uploads/2015/11/Understanding-by-Design-Expanded-2nd-Edition.pdf.

Woo, Wee Hong. 2016. "Using Gagne's Instructional Model in Phlebotomy Education." *Advances in Medical Education and Practice* 7: 511–15. doi:10.2147/AMEP.S110357.

Wu, Lin, Virginia Trotter Betts, Susan Jacob, Richard Nollan, and Tommie Norris. 2013. "Making Meaningful Connections: Evaluating an Embedded Librarian Pilot Project to Improve Nursing Scholarly Writing." *Journal of the Medical Library Association* 101, no. 4 (October): 323–26. https://doi.org/10.3163/1536-5050.101.4.016.

⑥ Further Reading

Barnett, Bill. 2012. "To Investigate Culture, Ask the Right Questions." *Harvard Business Review*, May 17, 2012. https://hbr.org/2012/05/to-investigate-culture-ask-the.

Burke, John, and Beth Tumbleson. 2011. "A Declaration of Embeddedness: Instructional Synergies and Sustaining Practices in LMS Embedded Librarianship." ACRL Conference. http://www.ala.org/acrl/sites/ala.org.acrl/files/content/conferences/confsandpreconfs/national/2011/papers/declaration_embedded.pdf.

Shumaker, David. 2009."Who Let the Librarians Out? Embedded Librarianship and the Library Manager." *Reference & User Services Quarterly* 48, no. 3: 239–42, 257. https://journals.ala.org/index.php/rusq/article/viewFile/3364/3610.

CHAPTER 8

Evaluating and Making Adjustments to Your Plan

THE EFFECTIVENESS OF AN EMBEDDED librarian action plan will be an important consideration in writing goals, project management, and communicating value. This plan must be viewed as a starting point, a dynamic proposal that must be flexible in design. It is important to understand that evaluating this plan regularly will help improve and strengthen the new embedded partnership. The library administration and senior management in the outside organization will need data to advocate for an embedded librarian program and determine if it is successful. Evidence of the impact made by an embedded librarian may be measured using quantitative or qualitative methodology. Setting measurable outcomes and evaluating an embedded librarian plan will also help all stakeholders make data-driven decisions about the sustainability of the new program.

Data should be at the center of strategic planning, as it provides information that helps answer key questions such as what to keep doing and what to stop doing. Criteria may be used to show the value of the librarian's efforts within an embedded program and point to ways for improved effectiveness. Data can help answer pressing questions and revise strategies. It may be used to demonstrate value-added services provided by the librarian within the embedded work group. For example, the embedded librarian has already performed a SWOT analysis, conducted reference interviews, and researched group needs for librarian assistance before writing the embedded program action plan. The cost of employing an informationist to perform research and analyze information needs is prohibitively expensive for most organizations. The embedded librarian's efforts in pulling together information and creating an action plan by itself demonstrates value. Continuing to evaluate the merits of an embedded program can establish the expertise of the librarian and the success of the partnership. Evaluation data may also be used to communicate how well the action plan is implemented while showing all participants where the program is having the most impact. It is important both to understand the role of evaluation within the embedded partnership and to discuss what should be evaluated.

The Role of Evaluation in the Embedded Librarian Program

Program evaluation is based on outcomes, which demonstrate the embedded librarian impact and inform decision-making. Embedding a librarian into any group creates organizational change. As Cowley (2007) illustrates in his article "Why Change Succeeds," it is important to build both formal and informal mechanisms and processes to make it work. Library administration and the embedded organization management must reinforce change with strategic planning and structures. The embedded librarian and the new partners must align work processes, build relationships, and put in the daily work. Data will show if the benefits outweigh the efforts. It is important to create a method for assessing progress that is more than anecdotal, as it may affect funding, staffing, and the sustainability of the program.

Evaluating the program will help establish what needs to be done and how to move forward. If data indicates some of the work is not getting the results needed, the embedded librarian may want to adjust the action plan or look at alternate data sources. The embedded partners may then use evaluation tools to better work together, creating new areas of focus within the program for improvement. For example, if the embedded partners send a monthly report to the outside organization outlining progress, a survey may indicate if anyone is actually reading these reports or if they are meaningful to the group. The partners may choose to give a quarterly presentation at a departmental meeting instead of continuing to write reports. Continually improving how embedded partners work together will help develop the working relationship. It will also entrench value alignment between the embedded organization and the library. These value milestones will assist in making nimble decisions based on planned outcomes and help determine what efforts to prioritize and continue.

The initial planning stages discussed in earlier chapters described an inquiry into the embedded partner goals and building shared embedded goals. It is important to discuss how to best gather data and manage both analysis and sharing processes. The embedded librarian must not only understand partner information needs, but also develop mutual processes for assessing that those needs are met.

The embedded librarian who provides needed services to the organization must strive to partner closely—both within the organization and in connecting the organization to the library—so that organizational responsibilities and accomplishments are shared as authentic partners. Evaluation is also central in communicating partnership touchpoints and mutual accolades. Results exhibit a shift from talk to engagement and may be used to tell a success story to stakeholders. Evaluation assists in learning the scope of both how well these needs are met and also how well both the embedded partner and the librarian understand what is essential within the organization.

Borden and Perkins developed a self-evaluation tool to assess the collaborative process. This process was designed to help partnerships observe different sides of problems and "constructively explore their differences ... [to] search for solutions" (1999). Elements examined in their "Collaboration Checklist" included how partners are connected, how catalysts are identified, and political systems or cultures (1999). Communication is essential to a synergistic partnership. Acknowledging and finding solutions to problems early in the liaison will set up the embedded librarian for success. Using various evaluation methods may help embedded groups move forward with new strategies and accomplish goals while strengthening their working relationship.

It is also important to determine where changes may be made easily and nimbly. The Borden and Perkins "Collaboration Checklist" (1999) is a recommended starting point to break down data points to examine. Several of these measurements are especially applicable for evaluating the embedded action plan. Key factors may be broken down to include:

- Outcome: the expected results of the embedded librarian program and why this matters
- Resources: the people identified to be involved, who will work to make the program a success, and what they have to work with—budget, tools, technology
- Timetable: a realistic timeline and clearly articulated milestones
- Measures: assessments of the embedded librarian's progress and success

Collaboration Outcome

The outcome—in other words, the visualization of the end product—is important. It is not only useful for identifying when goals have been reached, but it is also valuable to confirm that all participants have the same definition of success. The value of the embedded librarian within an organization may be demonstrated in reports and other tangible pieces that represent how information needs were met. Examples of reports include increased activity and interaction between the librarian, library staff, and the embedded group. It also may be exhibited in the librarian's knowledge of the community and how the embedded partnership contributed to the success of the organization (Long et al., 2012).

Desired outcomes may develop as the embedded librarian program progresses. For example, an embedded librarian working within an academic department may discover faculty have many questions about scholarly communication, specifically open access publishing. Faculty may have questions about peer-review processes for open access journals, and whether articles published should count toward tenure and promotion. Questions such as these may crop up in side conversations while the librarian and instructor are working together on different outcomes. The librarian may find him- or herself newly embedded as a member of the academic department's tenure committee, affecting timelines and creating new touchpoints for data analysis. Sharing outcomes and collaborating to create them will help cement the embedded partnership. Tracking these outcomes will help the embedded librarian evaluate effectiveness in communication and establishing shared goals.

Resources for Collaboration

Resources—including human elements—play a major role in an embedded librarian program. The librarian may plan to physically or virtually leave the library for embedded work, and resources plus time within the work schedule must be available to support efforts. The librarian and new partners will need the support of management to aid in coalition building and advocating changes needed to move forward. The embedded librarian acts as a non-competitive partner who works to help the organization reach its goals. The ability to serve as a neutral, supportive colleague boosts open communication and sharing. The librarian will need to plan for ample time to work with embedded partners and talk about new ways to resolve problems. If an embedded program is within an academic department, the librarian may find a quick faculty office visit may last hours longer, as other offices may be in close proximity. The librarian may be asked to discuss new projects as the librarian passes through the hallway. It is not uncommon for an embedded librarian to be asked to meet with faculty while the librarian is on another appointment. Working with new faculty and staying organized requires tracking and helps the librarian better entrench within the organization. The quality of the embedded librarian partnership may be evaluated by looking at how both the library and librarian are used as resources for the outside group. The quality of the embedded partnership collaboration may be examined by observing the librarian role as a commodity. Sharing insights from analyzed data in a meaningful way helps faculty view the embedded librarian as a vital resource within the organization. Identifying what should be evaluated assists the embedded collaborations to find the best next planning steps.

Collaboration Timelines

Establishing and adjusting a timeline with expected results and accountability can help steer new processes in the embedded organization as well as the supporting library. An effort to build a community of practice between the library and embedded organization may be assessed with milestones of library usage or increased instruction requests. The embedded librarian may want to track the scope of the program—is the librarian fully or partially embedded and how is that defined? Development of new communication systems, habits, and understandings must be continually appraised for timeliness, effectiveness, and understanding between the two groups.

Measuring Embedded Collaboration Progress

The role that evaluation plays in determining the best course of action in a successful embedded program is important. The librarian will want to begin the action plan implementation with a discussion about evaluating the effectiveness of the partnership. The embedded librarian and new partner will select what should be examined and tracked from the beginning. They will need to consider not only what to evaluate but also how to evaluate progress. New measures and evaluation tools may be needed. The librarian may discover new twists on traditional roles, leading to new strategies of engagement. Selecting what to evaluate also recognizes the resources, guidance, and expertise of the embedded librarian within the new partnership. Specific factors may vary according to the nature of the organization involved, but there are some basics that may be applied to any partnership.

ACTION PLAN AND OUTCOME FOR AN ACADEMIC LIBRARIAN

In this example the academic librarian wants to meet new faculty each semester—not only to introduce library resources and services, but also create an awareness of the services that an embedded librarian may bring to the table. Each component of this plan may be evaluated for improvement.

- Strategy—new faculty orientation
- Activity—individual appointments with new faculty
- Timeline—orientation completed by mid-semester for each new faculty member
- Partners—academic department chair, departmental faculty who are library champions
- Opportunity—help new faculty with research projects, advocate for embedded librarian activities within classes
- Threat—new faculty may not accept appointments, may not see the value of working with an embedded librarian
- Outcome—embedded librarian is able to meet with new faculty and integrate an information literacy student learning outcome within the curriculum of the course, if not this semester then by next semester

⊚ Evaluation Tools

There are several recommended tools available to evaluate an embedded librarian program. Program success is usually described in buzzwords such as goal attainment, establishing new cohorts, gaining credibility while communicating value, recognition from the target organization, having new partners demonstrate competency in newly learned information literacy skills, or concepts and sustainability. These descriptions are very positive but also very general terms, almost vague, by definition. Evaluation tools are useful for demonstrating value in more specific ways. It can be tricky to articulate to stakeholders what is working well within the embedded group if there is no planned assessment. Measured outcomes may be multi-dimensional and complex. Components that are measurable may include creating new procedures, solving problems with new partners, changing hierarchies or structures, mastering new skills, demonstrating an understanding of new concepts, empowering participants, and having increased library resources or services statistics. The embedded librarian does not need to create a new tool and may save time by using established evaluation models proven for use in other educational programs. Even if a specific tool does not completely match the needs for the embedded program's evaluation, it may be useful to simply adapt elements of an evaluation plan or several checklists already available in educational literature. These tools may be used to measure collaborations, processes, behaviors, and learning. There are numerous ways to evaluate the embedded program. Evaluation tools selected for discussion in this chapter include:

- VIPAT (Balsano et al., 2008)
- CIPP (Stufflebeam and Shinkfield, 2007)

- Four levels of learning evaluation (Kirkpatrick, 1998)
- Gagné's nine events of instruction (Gagné, Briggs, and Wager, 1992)

Measuring Collaborations

As discussed earlier in the chapter, Borden and Perkins created a self-evaluation tool to measure key factors that may help or hinder collaboration between extension groups. This tool uses a checklist to help examine both strengths and failings that may determine the success of a new or ongoing collaboration. The list of key factors tests participants' knowledge of the following factors: "communication, sustainability, research and evaluation, political climate, resources, catalysts, policies, history, connectedness, leadership, community development and understanding" (1999). Similar checklists may be created for evaluating an embedded librarian program using the Borden and Perkins article as a guideline. The librarian and new embedded partners may brainstorm to list what collaboration factors may be evaluated. Some of these elements may already be under way as a result of fact-finding needed to plan the embedded project.

Successful collaboration requires organizational flexibility. According to Brence (2010), there are a number of ways to create flexibility. One way is numerical flexibility—changing the organization's ability to adapt by changing the amount of labor hours to respond to needs. A second method of flexibility that Brence describes is functional—where employees perform different kinds of tasks, as needed, to accomplish the work. The second type of collaborative flexibility, where an embedded librarian or new partner may adapt roles to undertake new tasks, may also be used for evaluation. For example, the librarian may use librarian and faculty job descriptions, and each may make revisions or write new skills, experience, duties, responsibilities, and so forth as observed while the embedded program unfolds. Within an academic setting, the master syllabus may be collaboratively revised as well. The librarian may normally teach one information literacy session per course section and change responsibilities—becoming a regular guest lecturer within the course or the course management system.

While preparing to write the action plan, the librarian communicates with the outside organization, researches information needs, and evaluates these needs for feasibility and scope. Plans will include finding successful channels for collaboration to support partnerships. The library champions within the embedded organization may open doors to relationship building so that the embedded librarian fits into the group's politics, history, policies, and community. In a higher education institution, it works best if faculty and librarian act as true partners, bringing the spirit of equally regarded expertise into the equation. The embedded librarian hopes to become a recognized member of the outside organization and connect with leadership and partner colleagues. Relationship building is a priority but may be difficult to measure.

A checklist may be useful in evaluating how collaboration operates within the partnership, naming elements of intellectual capital or cognitive diversity the librarian brings to the organization. The librarian expertise in information organization, scholarly communication, publishing—and whether this expertise is useful in collaboration with faculty—may be measured. The roles assumed within the embedded organization may also be examined as contributing factors to success. The ACRL *Roles and Strengths of Teaching Librarians* (2017) may be used as factors in determining the success of the outcomes for the embedded librarian program. A percentage of time spent in the various roles of advocate, coordinator, instructional designer, leader, lifelong learner, teacher, and teaching partner (ACRL, 2017) may be measured in actual time spent or in percentages of roles, which may help quantify which combination leads to most success.

Another evaluation model that may be used to examine collaborations was developed by the Center for Innovation Management Studies (CIMS) at North Carolina University. The value innovation potential assessment tool (VIPAT) helps identify centers of influence who drive innovation within organizations, which may be used to define key collaborators for the embedded librarian. This tool uses a web-based survey with both qualitative and quantitative questions to assess readiness or roadblocks to business transformations. Understanding how change develops within the embedded organization as well as within the culture of the library is helpful. The librarian may more readily identify leaders and change agents who enable cultural change as well as those who inhibit change. The VIPAT analyzes nine organizational elements that may be measured as influences affecting innovation. According to an article by Balsano and colleagues, the three top indicators receiving the most attention for innovative businesses were open communication, empowerment, and risk taking. "This tool's value may lie more in its role as an enabler of internal discussions of innovation . . . it engages the innovative potential in all employees to generate high-impact ideas that can be implemented to generate value" (2008: 32).

The VIPAT tool development is outlined in a 2005 article that describes empowerment culture as one where "skilled people have ownership to innovate in their area" (Aiman-Smith et al., 2005: 39). Empowerment culture, both within the embedded organization and the supporting library, allows the embedded librarian to collaborate openly with embedded partners and independently identify and address issues using library services and resources. Empowerment, open communication, and risk taking are important factors that contribute to collaboration. These are terms that may be difficult to define. Content validity, defined as how well concepts are described in concrete language, may be demonstrated using the VIPAT tool, as it uses statements that reflect intended definitions. Validity refers to the degree to which items in a survey accurately measure what is intended to be measured. The VIPAT tool is available using the Aiman-Smith article and is recommended for continually measuring and identifying key players for an embedded librarian collaboration.

Evaluating Processes: CIPP Evaluation Model

Another evaluation tool, the CIPP evaluation model, is commonly used to help measure educational program effectiveness. This program assessment was developed from the 1960s to 1970s by Stufflebeam, who first created a "primitive checklist" at Ohio State used in Ohio public schools, which later became the CIPP evaluation model. CIPP is linked to professional standards, accountability, and improvement (Stufflebeam and Shinkfield, 2007). It links evaluation with the decision-making process, and Stufflebeam used feedback from educational partners and stakeholders to make a checklist with accountability in mind. The CIPP model provides stakeholders with summative answers to their most pressing questions. It also helps operationalize the program being evaluated, determining—what next?—steps that may be taken to improve outcomes (Stufflebeam, 2001). An embedded librarian may use the CIPP evaluation model to provide long-term important evaluative reports to both embedded partners and library stakeholders. It may be used to analyze "impact, effectiveness, sustainability and transportability" for embedded librarian processes or methods (Stufflebeam, 2007).

The CIPP model evaluates content, input, process, and product. It can be used during any stage of an embedded librarian program and is very helpful in making decisions throughout the stages of any long-term project, based on analysis of improvements. It may be used to examine processes to identify successful outcomes and failures. Key questions attached to CIPP include the following:

1. Context: What needs to be done? (goals)
2. Input: How should it be done? (strategies)
3. Process: Is it being done? (activities)
4. Product: Did it succeed? (outcomes)

In the product section of the evaluation process, the success of a program may be assessed by examining its "impact, effectiveness, sustainability and transportability" (Stufflebeam and Shinkfield, 2007).

Applying the CIPP evaluation model to an embedded librarian program is most effective following the SWOT analysis on both the outside organization and library services, and after initial outreach efforts have helped identify first steps in the embedding process. Formative assessment takes place in the process component of CIPP, and summative assessment occurs in the product part. CIPP assists in staying on track and helps avoid being sidetracked within the embedding process. The CIPP model used with an evaluation checklist creates documents that may be used to communicate the value of an embedded librarian program to major stakeholders and to meet accountability needs. If this checklist is made available as a spreadsheet-type document, it can be very useful in communicating large pieces of information in a simpler format. It can also be used to clearly indicate where improvements are recommended for strategies and activities in order to lead to better outcomes.

The CIPP evaluation checklist helps identify needs for library services and may be used to guide the implementation process of specific strategies designed by the embedded librarian to provide these services. It also provides information to improve cost effectiveness versus value-added librarian efforts.

Context

The context evaluation assists in assessing the readiness for an embedded librarian program. The SWOT analysis helps identify opportunities, but context helps assess whether the outside organization is attuned to its own information needs. These needs are diagnosed and goals are selected.

Input

The input evaluation identifies strategic collaborations and plans to implement embedded librarian goals. Potential initial approaches are examined, and a plan may be formulated for steps related to the embedded librarian plan. Alternate approaches are included in the analysis, and relevance to the needs of the embedded group is important. These approaches may easily be discovered with a literature review of embedded librarian case studies. The input evaluation helps determine the best use of resources, including the human resources needed to implement an embedded librarian program. The input component should be mutually beneficial to the outside organization and library services.

Process

The process evaluation occurs periodically during the project to observe the practicality and effectiveness of the embedded librarian's activities. Documentation of strategies and outcomes is a key component in this part of the program evaluation. This documentation includes successes and failures, as well as in-process changes of direction and barriers encountered. Costs are tracked and feedback is collected from the outside organization members who directly benefit from the role of the embedded librarian within their group. The process evaluation is vital to embedded librarian work and should be recognized as a priority for time management.

Product

The product evaluation accesses the outcomes of the program, using both unexpected and hoped-for results. The product may include focus group feedback, testimonials, achievements, cohort comparisons, or any other program results that demonstrate outcomes related to the efforts of the embedded librarian.

All parts of the CIPP model include continuous monitoring, solicitation of interactive feedback (formal and informal), and reflective observation during the process and after the program is completed. The goal of the entire evaluation is continuous improvement of both the process and product. The advantage of using the CIPP model is that it provides a careful analysis of the processes used to embed the librarian. It helps to look closely not only at the end product, but also to learn what is the best way to move forward and make the process mutually beneficial.

Scope Evaluation of the Embedded Program: Four Levels of Learning Evaluation

A third evaluation model that may be helpful in beginning an embedded librarian program is the four levels of learning evaluation defined by Kirkpatrick in his 1998 book *Evaluating Training Programs: The Four Levels*. The four levels are reaction, learning, behavior, and results. This evaluation model is useful for training and preparing the librarian to undertake the new role as an embedded librarian.

Reactions include what the librarian wants to learn, comments, and suggestions. The librarian may also want to use this model to follow up preliminary conversations with proposed partners. An informal survey may be used to see if the meeting was useful to the new partners.

The learning level evaluates knowledge and skills, and the development of new skills and attitudes. An embedded librarian may want to incorporate a learning activity into starter conversations both to evaluate the prior knowledge of the embedded group and to credential the librarian.

The behavior level defines the extent to which a change in behavior has occurred during the training process. This step in the Kirkpatrick model is especially useful as the partners begin to work with each other. Behaviors, job duties, and how the librarian works within the embedded organization may be noted and tracked to see if these changes should be sustained over time.

The results level may include increased patron interaction, improved reference, outreach or instructional work quality, retention, or greater job satisfaction.

This evaluation model is also useful in discovering how much the embedded group has learned from their association with the librarian. Did they develop new skills or new attitudes about information or digital literacy? Has their information-seeking behavior changed? Does the embedded librarian relationship benefit members of the outside organization? Do they ask for more interaction opportunities with the librarian? Are they using more library services and resources than before? Are they aware that the librarian's embedded relationship has resulted in changes in their behavior?

Gagné's Nine Events of Instruction

Another excellent tool, Gagné's nine events of instruction, may be used to evaluate engagement within the organization for the embedded librarian. This instructional design tool is effective in academic embedded programs and examines the impact of an embedded librarian. It may be used for instructional design and works well in designing content for developing an embedded librarian program. Following are the nine events described by Gagné, Briggs, and Wager (1992: 190):

1. Gain the attention of the students.
2. Inform students of the objectives.
3. Stimulate recall of prior learning.
4. Present the content.
5. Provide learning guidance.
6. Elicit performance (practice).
7. Provide feedback.
8. Assess performance.
9. Enhance retention and transfer to the job.

The design of instruction delivery for an embedded librarian may include both integrated courses for students and faculty development in academic programs. Gagné's nine events build upon each other to construct a product that behaves very differently after learning, and this model is a good tool to demonstrate the transformative nature of any effective embedded librarian program. The embedded librarian creates new library champions, a process that helps to develop the embedded program. As the librarian develops a culture of information literacy within the organization, it becomes much easier to establish new relationships and perpetuate the embedded model within the organization.

More informal evaluation tools may be used, such as polls and surveys, to see if the embedded librarian's work is sustainable and transportable. An embedded librarian creates strong relationships within the organization that continue, even if another librarian replaces the original.

Sustaining the Embedded Librarian Model with Evidence

The sustainability of any embedded librarian plan may be defined as its capacity for ongoing work, organic relationship growth, and maintaining effective movements for change and collaboration. It involves long-term stakeholder/administration buy-in as well as the development of a community of practice that can sustain a mutually beneficial partnership with the library. Evidence of this mutual benefit helps support efforts and show growth and innovation. Frequent library staff communications, especially identifying their contributions to the success of the embedded program, is important to sustain efforts. Transparency will also help library staff, who may not be actively involved day to day in the embedded librarian program, to understand its value and support the embedded librarian's efforts.

Successful embedded librarian programs increase library resource usage, and staff services may be in higher demand. Administration must clearly recognize staff who will assist with increased library services, desk interactions, and questions resulting from the embedded organization. Sharing the results of evaluating the embedded librarian program externally and internally contributes to sustainability as it increases library visibility, eliminates silos, and develops a shared knowledge culture. This type of culture must be given an opportunity to develop naturally so that the partnership is integral to both the library and the embedded group.

Visibility and Sustainability

As the librarian and embedded partners formally evaluate components of their work, sharing the results increases visibility for both groups. It establishes team contributions and resources that contribute to success factors and strengthens the embedded library brand. The embedded librarian program cannot operate without the support of library staff, and it is beneficial to involve them in both failures and successes. Shared knowledge cements trust and focuses staff from both the library and embedded organization on shared values and goals. Transparency may be as simple as sharing takeaways from embedded partner meetings and why others may find information applicable or relevant. For example, an embedded health sciences librarian may share the results of a clinical team-teaching session using various library databases for decision-making. Use of these resources may prompt stories of how library resources may be used to help patients, and this shared information supports health clinicians, library staff who select resources, library management who secure funding, and the embedded librarian. As efforts from the partnership become visible, it helps eliminate duplication of efforts and improves work quality. It also reiterates the human elements needed to support the embedded librarian and organizational partners.

Eliminating Silos for Sustaining the Embedded Librarian Program

Evaluating the embedded librarian project can help break down silos between work groups. Sharing may encourage more connectedness between the library and embedded organization. If a library staff person working at the public services desk reads a brief report about how the embedded librarian is working with a professor, the staff may feel more connected when that instructor seeks help. This strengthened sense of alignment helps nurture the embedded coalition, making the embedded partners feel welcomed within the library spaces. Staff may feel empowered to use or build upon the embedded librarian's work by acknowledging organizational milestones and recognizing the role they play in providing needed services to these partners. Sharing the progress of the program by sharing evaluation results also creates organizational commitment to cultural changes within the embedded organization (Clobridge, 2017).

Librarians who are embedded serve an important role in organizations, providing unbiased, objective approaches to evaluating research and information activities. Embedded librarians who work as committee members within the embedded group provide different perspectives, help bridge silos, and connect different groups. Sharing information about how the librarian chooses to evaluate the embedded program may help other groups and communicate the embedded librarian expertise. It is not uncommon within a university for different work groups to discuss initiatives that are already in progress across campus. The embedded librarian may use knowledge of evaluation tools to help eliminate barriers, bringing groups together to innovate, develop, and evaluate new programs for student success and retention.

Developing a Shared Knowledge Culture

Once embedded strategies are outlined and evaluated, shared knowledge and a determination to create new opportunities for sharing may help accelerate cultural change within the embedded organization. It may help key partners move from planning to action. As successful outcomes are identified through evaluation, staff morale increases and word of the accomplishments spreads. Sharing openly, reaching many people within the embedded group, can reach new potential partners. In organizations where the shared evaluation results show impact, embedded librarians may be in greater demand. The library may need to hire new staff to support the embedded program. Another possibility within academic departments is that other departments may want to embed a librarian. New hires may be needed to fulfill this call for embedded librarians.

As the knowledge grows about how embedded librarians add value to academic departments, it will be important to establish the transportability of the action plan with continuing communication and training within library staff. The embedded librarian program must be sustainable so that another librarian could continue the work, if necessary. Should the librarian leading the new program be unable to continue working with the outside organization, it is important to be able to train a replacement to easily step into the original librarian's shoes. Evaluation tools and analyzed data will help improve this process and tell a story of what efforts had the most impact and best outcomes for the embedded organization.

⊚ Key Points

This chapter has discussed the role of evaluation within the embedded librarian program and the value of the evaluation process. Various tools and data points are suggested to collect and analyze data. Adjustments may be made and justified with more data interpretation. Integrating these recommended evaluation tools in this chapter will help deliver evidence of the effectiveness and value of the embedded librarian program.

- VIPAT (Balsano et al., 2008)—to identify change agents and possible embedded partners within the outside organization for the embedded librarian
- CIPP (Stufflebeam and Shinkfield, 2007)—to show the impact and sustainability of the embedded librarian program, demonstrate effectiveness and transportability of the work performed by embedded librarian, and improve the program
- Four levels of learning evaluation (Kirkpatrick, 1998)—to evaluate training and demonstrate value-added services for the embedded librarian program

- Gagné's nine events of instruction (Gagné, Briggs, and Wager, 1992)—to improve embedded librarian pedagogical techniques within an academic embedded program and outreach presentations for any type of embedded program

An evaluation process demonstrates impact and value-added embedded librarian services, and cements coalitions. Using a variety of evaluation tools produces valid evidence of embedded librarian efficacy and aids in the librarian learning process.

The next chapter will discuss key technology tools and expert embedded librarian services that will help the librarian become a leader within the embedded organization.

References

ACRL (Association of College and Research Libraries). 2017. *Roles and Strengths of Teaching Librarians.* American Library Association. April 28, 2017. http://www.ala.org/acrl/standards/teachinglibrarians.

Aiman-Smith, Lynda, Nina Goodrich, David Roberts, and James Scinta. 2005. "Assessing Your Organization's Potential for Value Innovation." *Research-Technology Management* 48, no. 2: 35–42. https://doi.org/10.1080/08956308.2005.11657303.

Balsano, Thomas J., Nina E. Goodrich, Richard K. Lee, John W. Miley, Terri F. Morse, and David A. Roberts. 2008. "Identify Your Innovation Enablers and Inhibitors." *Research-Technology Management* 51, no. 6: 23–33. https://doi.org/10.1080/08956308.2008.11657534.

Borden, Lynne M., and Daniel F. Perkins. 1999. "Assessing Your Collaboration: A Self Evaluation Tool." *Journal of Extension* 37, no. 2 (April). https://www.joe.org/joe/1999april/tt1.php.

Brence, Ieva. 2010. "Organisational Flexibility and Possibilities for Its Assessment." *Journal of Business Management* no. 3: 105–14. *Business Source Complete*, EBSCO*host*.

Clobridge, Abby. 2017. "40 Reasons to Share Your Knowledge." *Online Searcher* 41, no. 5: 63–65. http://www.infotoday.com/OnlineSearcher/Articles/The-Open-Road/-Reasons-to-Share-Your-Knowledge-120283.shtml.

Cowley, Bill. 2007. "'Why Change Succeeds': An Organizational Self-Assessment." *Organization Development Journal* 25, no. 1: 25–30. *Business Source Complete*, EBSCO*host*.

Gagné, Robert, Leslie J. Briggs, and Walter W. Wager. 1992. *Principles of Instructional Design.* 4th ed. Fort Worth, TX: Harcourt Brace College. https://www.hcs64.com/files/Principles%20of%20instructional%20design.pdf.

Kirkpatrick, Donald L. 1998. *Evaluating Training Programs: The Four Levels.* 2nd ed. San Francisco: Berrett-Koehler.

Long, Amy, Colbe Galston, Elizabeth Kelsen Huber, and Katherine Johnson. 2012. "Community Reference: Making Libraries Indispensable in a New Way." *American Libraries*, June 13, 2012. https://americanlibrariesmagazine.org/2012/06/13/community-reference-making-libraries-indispensable-in-a-new-way/.

Stufflebeam, Daniel L. 2001. "Evaluation Checklists: Practical Tools for Guiding and Judging Evaluations." *American Journal of Evaluation* 22, no. 1: 71–79. https://doi.org/10.1177/109821400102200107.

———. 2007. "CIPP Evaluation Model Checklist, Second Edition: A Tool for Applying the CIPP Model to Assess Long-Term Enterprises." Western Michigan University. March 17, 2007. https://www.wmich.edu/sites/default/files/attachments/u350/2014/cippchecklist_mar07.pdf.

Stufflebeam, Daniel L., and Anthony L. Shinkfield. 2007. *Evaluation Theory, Models and Applications.* San Francisco: Jossey-Bass.

⊚ Further Reading

Almeida, Nora, and Julia Pollack. 2017. "In Bed with the Library: A Critical Exploration of Embedded Librarianship at the City University New York." *Communications in Information Literacy* 11, no. 1: 122–26. https://doi.org/10.15760/comminfolit.2017.11.1.38.

Mears, Kim, Maryska Connolly-Brown, Julie K. Gaines, Lindsay Blake, Kathy Davies, Peter Shipman, and Gail Kouame. 2017. "Evaluation of an Embedded Program through the Embedded Ecosystem Framework and Toolkit." *Journal of Academic Librarianship* 43, no. 6: 532–39. https://doi.org/10.1016/j.acalib.2017.07.001.

Northern Illinois University Faculty Development and Instructional Design Center. 2017. "Gagné's Nine Events of Instruction." Accessed December 28, 2017. http://www.niu.edu/facdev/_pdf/guide/learning/gagnes_nine_events_instruction.pdf.

Stuart, Ansley. 2017. "Embedded Librarianship: The Future of Libraries." *OUPblog*. July 18, 2017. https://blog.oup.com/2017/07/medical-library-resources/.

CHAPTER 9

Using Combined Technology and Expert Services in Your Plan

SUCCESSFULLY EMBEDDED LIBRARIANS find much job satisfaction and undertake many challenges as they work within the embedded group. Librarians who describe why they find this type of role to be so rewarding often say that they enjoy being able to use the skills, competencies, and knowledge base they have developed to make a positive impact as an embedded librarian. An article by Schulte states, "Traditional librarians and embedded librarians were actually participating in similar activities . . . using their [expertise] . . . within their organization . . . to be truly embedded" (2012: 125). Embedded librarians go where the action is, bringing not only library resources and services to the attention of the user group but also unique librarian expertise. Embedded librarian competencies include a technology skill set combined with expert knowledge of information science, creating a unique, strong, and needed presence within the outside organization. This chapter will guide you through some of the ways that an embedded librarian may use a librarian technology skill set and knowledge base to establish leadership status within the role as an embedded librarian.

Learning how to wisely use technology as a tool in the embedded librarian action plan is a smart approach. Collaborative technology helps librarians work beyond library walls both virtually and while working within physical spaces of an embedded program. These tools also assist with overcoming obstacles to an embedded program where library staffing may limit how often an embedded librarian may visit an outside department or organization. Productive technology expertise requires both a determination to become a more fluent tool user and a playful curiosity for exploring emerging technologies. Academic and health sciences librarians may find success by embedding themselves into the institutional courseware as a teaching partner.

Course or Learning Management Systems (CMSs or LMSs)

Academic librarians who are embedded within courses and academic programs frequently partner with faculty who teach online or hybrid courses. Effective embeddedness may lead to helping to redesign course content, instructional delivery, or even an academic program curriculum. An embedded academic project described by Thomas and McIntosh gave the embedded librarian a better understanding of an online course by regular access to a communication course in Blackboard. Technology tools used within the course Blackboard site included a LibGuide with "resources, search strategies, and citation guidance tailored specifically to the assignments of the course [plus] . . . contact information for the embedded librarian" (2013). The librarian also used various components within Blackboard to read assignments and post announcements that went to student email accounts. The librarian also posted links to library resources and participated in student discussion boards. The instructor and librarian collaborated to revise course content at the end of the academic term to address information gaps identified by a student survey. Improved instruction and information on topic development and identifying keywords were added to the LibGuide. This example shows how technology used in Blackboard and LibGuides may lead to richer teaching collaborations and improving course design.

There are many advantages to learning to use course management systems (CMSs). They are easy to use and have robust help features. If a librarian is embedded within a course and the course instructor uses a CMS, the librarian must work together with the instructor to embed both the librarian and the materials used by the librarian within the course. Most, if not all, of the course materials are located within the CMS, making it easy for students to use a single system to both navigate and engage with the materials and teaching partners. The students and course instructor will not have to be reminded to go to the library website to contact the embedded librarian. Both the librarian and assignment-specific resources are readily available within the same area where students and the instructor are working. If the class is hybrid, the students will have a familiar face on campus as well to contact for assistance. The embedded librarian may provide students with customizable librarian services, helping students succeed during their academic term. Duke University Libraries has a unique embedded librarian program where librarians are embedded within the residence halls for first-year students. As stated by the Duke Residence Hall Program website, the "Residence Hall Librarian is the first-year student's go-to person for any questions about the Libraries in general or about research needs in particular" (Duke University Libraries, 2018). The embedded librarian within course management systems plays exactly the same role—virtually. The librarian and instructor define that role, the research services go-to person, within the CMS.

Use of courseware technology is not limited to academic embedded librarians. School librarians, health sciences librarians, and special librarians may be embedded in school courseware, but academic pursuits are not the only options. Workshops, webinars, and other online instruction may be embedded within other organization intranets or online groups. Public and government librarians may become embedded in teaching classes with community partners or partner with school librarians, using freely available versions of courseware or simply components commonly found within CMSs. The creative use of library websites, LibGuides, and freely available applications such as Google apps may work well in developing continuing education, technology or vocational workshops, and webinars, rather than only offering face-to-face classroom instruction. The possibilities multiply when using courseware, and learning how to use the software is both easy and intuitive.

Most of these systems have the same components such as announcements, a course home page, discussion boards, and ways to organize content into folders or units. Academic librarians, school librarians, and medical librarians who are embedded in courses or academic/health sciences departments are frequently expected to possess Blackboard-type technology expertise. Using these learning software systems meets the users where they already are working, rather than expecting them to leave the site to access librarian assistance or library resources. An embedded librarian may assist with CMS course design and the strategic placement of tutorials, links to resources, and curated research assistance, providing important information at the student point of need. Braun (2016) describes basic steps in design thinking, which the embedded librarian may want to use to work with the course instructor: determine a problem that needs to be solved, discuss alternatives, and develop potential solutions for testing. For example, students may have a persuasive essay to write for an English class, but the course instructor may feel the sources found are not scholarly. The embedded librarian partner and instructor may brainstorm together and discuss new ways to design instruction within the CMS to help the students learn how to rate the quality of a resource, using a rubric. CMS tools, such as multiple-choice quizzes that self-grade, may also be used to test understanding of evaluating information concepts.

There are many CMS tools that the embedded librarian may use in addition to self-graded quizzes. Following are examples of library resources that may be linked within an online course:

- How to contact the librarian for help
- Link to 24/7 chat assistance
- Quick links to key databases, not the entire library database collection
- Tutorials for choosing a topic, identifying keywords, search techniques
- Checklists for evaluating information
- Citation documentation
- Subject LibGuide or class guide

An excellent resource for the embedded librarian to use in online course design is the Quality Matters (QM) course design rubric standards for higher ed course design. QM is a peer-reviewed process used to evaluate the quality of online and hybrid instruction design. The rubric for higher education includes these eight general standards:

1. Course Overview and Introduction
2. Learning Objectives (Competencies)
3. Assessment and Measurement
4. Instructional Materials
5. Course Activities and Learner Interaction
6. Learner Support
7. Accessibility and Usability

(Quality Matters, 2014)

The course overview and introduction are usually located on the course home page. Most higher educational institutions include a link to the library and a resources section. These areas within the CMS are useful to both faculty and the student as they organize the information as a section within the course space, meeting these library users within the course. It makes it easy to use library resources without leaving the CMS, saving the time of the users. The embedded librarian and faculty partner may also use this space to define the role of the librarian within the course, introduce both partners, and communicate contact details. This is also a good place to include some introductory tutorials or instructional tools (LibGuides, for example) to gain the attention of the student and reinforce the concept of the embedded librarian as teaching partner.

The learning objectives for the course are typically identified in the course syllabus. The course instructor and embedded librarian will want to collaborate to include information literacy (IL) student learning outcomes (SLOs). The instructor may want to identify IL SLOs for which the librarian will be responsible for teaching, or simply list them within the syllabus with no specifically assigned teacher.

Assessment and measurement, including a description of grading, are also typically described within the syllabus. The embedded librarian and instructor may design instructional assessments and include these as part of the total grade. For example, students may complete a tutorial with a graded quiz and upload the grade reports to the CMS for a part of their course grade. If the librarian is not listed as a course instructor within the course catalog, it is important that the embedded role does not include grading assignments or making pass/fail decisions. However, that does not mean that the embedded librarian cannot create or collaborate to create assignments and help design how IL SLOs are measured within the course.

Instructional materials contributed by the librarian may be presented as a unit within the course calendar or set up to be asynchronous tools, available when needed by the student. Examples of instruction may use various course tools, such as Blackboard Collaborate, voice-over PowerPoint, voice-over PDF (Camtasia), brief tutorials, LibGuides, and various handouts such as citation documentation guides. The type of technology used for instructional tools may be varied, but most will be similar to the same ones used for IL classroom teaching sessions. The embedded librarian, in hybrid classroom courses with face-to-face IL teaching sessions, may use this technology for flipped classroom and various other active learning scenarios used for both online and hybrid courses. According to Clifton and Jo, the flipped classroom "provides opportunities for peer-to-peer learning . . . synonymous with cooperative and collaborative learning, [improving] . . . inter-professional communication and growth [skills]" (2016: 314). Students receive instruction and may practice activities online before face-to-face instruction. During the embedded librarian–led classroom instruction, the librarian may work directly with students to gain a better understanding of student information needs and questions. The flipped classroom model works well within the embedded librarian course model, as it helps students actively develop their understanding of IL concepts. According to the Edudemic.com *Teacher's Guides* (2017), using the flipped classroom shifts the passive model of learning (viewing lectures, reading) to students engaging in hands-on learning. Various supplemental tools are also available for learning how best to assist student information needs in fully online courses.

Samples of technology used to supplement instructional materials include polling software or group discussion boards. These learning tools may be used for learning activities and interaction with concepts. The CMS may be used to form groups to work together within the courseware to reinforce learning and improve understanding of concepts. Groups may use CMS tools such as whiteboards or wikiboards to communicate and share ideas. Links to librarian help or 24/7 chat may be embedded within the CMS group areas, wikiboards, whiteboard, or other areas to get assistance to questions as needed.

Learner support embedded at fail points and within various technologies within the CMS make a difference. Students are encouraged to ask questions and use these tools extensively when they are strategically placed within course materials. The embedded librarian will also gain insight about the usability as well as accessibility of the instructional tools, if help is readily available as part of these materials.

According to Clifton and Jo, the benefits of embedded librarianship within the hybrid instruction model "show improvement in instruction through peer-group or collaborative mentoring and different contributions to content" (2016: 308). The synergy of working together as collaborators and course designers benefits the embedded academic department for better course and curriculum design. Shared knowledge for content design and tech tools helps both teaching partners learn from each other. The experiences gained help develop insights into teaching other disciplines for the embedded librarian as well as other courses for the embedded group.

A newly embedded librarian may find time management an issue in scheduling teaching collaboration time. Libraries with staffing issues as well as academic departments with few full-time faculty may find an embedded project challenging. The librarian may lead as a communication facilitator using various channels and tools.

Communication Tech Tools

Embedded librarians who regularly leave the library to work with partners in an outside organization must consistently communicate with library administration and develop ways to perform job duties at a distance. Many librarians use mobile technology to accomplish these tasks—using smartphones, tablets, or laptops to stay in touch with their libraries while they are working beyond library walls. These same librarians use similar tools to communicate with partners within embedded communities whenever they return to the library. If the librarian beginning an embedded librarian role is not able to leave the library physically, many of these same tools may be used to effectively communicate within a virtually embedded program. Because librarians may be using various devices to perform their work, there is an expectation for the librarian to have a high level of software proficiency. Embedded librarians often possess a lifelong interest in new tech. Technology tools are expected to be synchronized, up to date, interoperable between platforms, and easy to use. Since most of these tools require an internet connection, anticipation for and dealing with connectivity problems is another skill needed to do this type of embedded outreach work. Instruction librarians as well as librarians presenting at conferences often exchange ideas about coping with technology issues.

Solo librarians and those who work in under-staffed library environments may find that they are be able to work as an embedded librarian using virtual communication, instructional, or collaborative tools. These tools allow these librarians to overcome staffing barriers to embedded work. Thorough fact-finding and questioning is important for operating in a virtual embedded environment, and it may be a more effective way for these librarians to embed an outside group. Important collaborative features needed include the following:

- Messaging or chat
- Content or file sharing
- Video or voice communications

(Smith, 2017)

It is very important to find out what the embedded group is already using to collaborate. There is no reason to reinvent the wheel, but if the group is only using emails to collaborate, this opportunity may help the group view the librarian as a leader for tech tools in this area.

Working the embedded librarian action plan effectively for both solo librarians who find it difficult to leave the library and those who physically leave the library walls will include the smart use of virtual collaboration and communication tools. It is important to anticipate which tool(s) will work best and save both the time of the librarian and library administration as well as best serve the time constraints of the embedded organization.

Research carefully how the outside group communicates. It may be unrealistic to expect an organization to use a new communication tool solely to stay in touch with an embedded librarian partner, but that doesn't mean the outside partner would not be interested in learning about the tool. Conversely, it may be unrealistic to ask library administration to make a major change in how it communicates with one librarian, but introducing new ways to stay in touch may benefit the library as a whole. Following are some examples of the types of software that may be used, and the textbox includes some free video conferencing software tools as noted by *PC Magazine*.

- Video conferencing—including desktop sharing—for small groups of two to six
- Chat or text-messaging tools—for short question and answer sessions
- Virtual meeting tools—software that accommodates larger groups in a webinar setting

---

FREE VIDEO CONFERENCING SOFTWARE

Skillful and intelligent use of virtual communication is important and may positively impact both the library and the embedded group. *PC Magazine* lists the top video conferencing software tools each summer. The August 2017 list with free versions includes the following:

- RingCentral
- Zoho Meeting
- Skype
- Join.me
- Amazon Chime
- GoToMeeting
- Cisco WebEx

(Martinez and McLaughlin, 2017)

Virtual Meetings with Embedded Partners

Video conferencing tools include various capabilities and may be used within a CMS to answer reference questions. They offer more than face-to-face interactions. Tools may include desktop sharing, whiteboard tools, in-app chat, and the ability to record either audio or video to share the meeting with others later. The embedded librarian may offer office hours or hold a virtual workshop that may be recorded and shared with the class in case others are also having similar difficulties with a research assignment.

Joint projects may also be accomplished either within the context of a virtual meeting or simply as asynchronous document or spreadsheet collaborations. Free and fee-based collaboration and productivity tools may be used when the librarian and embedded partners cannot physically meet. Shared documents, spreadsheets, slides, files, videos, and images may convey a lot of information with a relatively short delivery time. These technology tools are important for staying in touch, developing programs, and conducting library services outreach. Using technology tools as a part of the embedded librarian collaboration conveys credibility, expertise, and visibility. Academic libraries may also have access to institutional content management systems, course learning software, and faculty development workshops to develop new means for virtually shared work and communication. These tools are not limited to use within the embedded librarian realm. The ability to have embedded partner meetings, meeting with other library staff, and cross-disciplinary collaborations may also be explored. It is possible to work collaboratively across institutions as well, sharing embedded librarian technology expertise well beyond the individual embedded project. There are both commercial and academic software programs developed for these types of projects.

Diverse teams from different backgrounds maximize innovative idea sharing and work well in collaborative research teams. When these groups include embedded librarians, these participants make contributions to clinical research as well as data management efforts.

An example of this type group was the VIVO team—"collaborators on an American Recovery and Reinvestment Act funded project from the National Institutes of Health (NIH) to the University of Florida" (Garcia-Milian et al., 2013). The VIVO program, a team science collaboration platform developed by Cornell University, involved a group sharing interaction within different disciplines and research teams, many of which included embedded librarians. Use of technologies for facilitating group work requires that the embedded librarian not only learn how to use the technology but also remain flexible and try to experiment. Multi-disciplinary projects are great opportunities for embedded librarians. Knowledge of the research process, scholarly communication, data management, and project management within the library translates well into cross-disciplinary work. Librarians may demonstrate the value of their expertise and also emerge as leaders in the use of tech tools in learning, research, and other collaborative activities.

Establishing a Leadership Role within the Outside Organization

Librarians regularly use and evaluate a variety of technology tools in providing information services for instructive reference, collection development, and staff communication. They also provide assistance to library patrons who need help in learning to use newly acquired devices and software. For this reason, most librarians consistently work to improve and develop hardware and software competencies. Examples of proficiencies expected to be used on the job at any type of library include virtual chat, tutorial instructional design, and acquiring new materials using a vendor software platform.

Embedded Librarians as Emerging Technology Leaders

Many librarians are early adopters of emerging technologies. The embedded librarian may bring a wide range of technology knowledge to the table within the outside organization. The ability to use technology effectively is viewed as a basic skill in a librarian job description. Most job interviews for librarian positions at any type of library include questions about technology tool experience, including emerging technologies. Experience with instructional design, new social media, ILS, and CMS platforms are often listed as preferred skills in job postings. Examples of technology expertise may range from use of social media to knowledge of website design and website/tutorial usability or UX (user experience).

Embedded librarians serve as a resource to outside organizations to research benchmarking data for decision-making. Reference search strategies and database search skills translate well to this type of research request. Embedded librarians within the corporate sector may be asked to help HR with benchmarking job descriptions, best practices, background research, and information about software vendors (Nagarkar and Murari, 2010). The embedded librarian may perform research using many different sources, open access and institutional. Familiarity with search engines and the nimble use of widely different search engines contributes value-added services to the embedded organization.

Most library services are delivered using some type of technology. Quality information retrieval depends on knowledge of the technology used to organize and classify information. Some of the most popular professional development sessions at library conferences include learning about new software to use for services, instruction, assessment, community outreach, and collaboration. And some of the most active conversations on professional Listservs include questions about which tool or software is recommended for use in collaboration, to perform a specific job, or to provide a service. For example, the use of LibGuides for instruction, a technology developed by Springshare, is a frequently occurring hot topic on the ALA instruction Listserv (http://lists.ala.org/sympa/info/ili-l). LibGuides are used for assessment, instructional design, virtual help, and much more. Librarians actively work to vet such tools and make buying decisions concerning various library technologies as a normal job duty. Purchasing technology may also include both simple and complex knowledge of licensing for use. For this reason, knowledge of how to evaluate not only information retrieved but also the technology that delivers this information is a core competency that sets job candidates apart from each other.

This skills expectation is one of the elements that help to set librarians apart while working to embed another organization. Librarians deal with technology issues regularly—dealing with vendors, interoperability between platforms, rapidly changing software, and so forth. Leadership skills in communication, decision-making, troubleshooting, and project management have been included as part of the librarian job description at most public, academic, school, and special library job postings. Professional development available at library conferences includes inclusive thinking and staying up to date with technology and emerging technologies. Collection development and acquisition skills for librarians include the purchase of database, instructional software, and makerspace tools.

Expectations for Technology Leadership

Librarians are often called upon to be leaders within their communities because of their expert knowledge in using and selecting technology tools. Most libraries provide virtual assistance for patrons after "normal" working hours in addition to phone or in-person reference staffing. Examples of such assistance include anything from a list of FAQs on the website, to instructional videos and printable instructions, to chat reference or a way to email a question.

The ability for a library to provide these access methods requires staff to evaluate and select appropriate virtual tools utilizing a set of criteria. Such criteria usually include:

- Usability—how friendly to use are these tools?
- Intuitiveness—can the tool be used with little or no instruction?
- Stability—will the tool stand up to heavy use?

Tool purchases are discussed across library departments and often benchmarked by observing how the technology is used by other libraries. This mindful and collaborative method for selecting new library software is an important proficiency for an embedded librarian.

A valuable question that may be used in the initial stages of beginning an embedded librarian program could be any of the following:

- How do you evaluate technology tools?
- How do you evaluate the information you find in using these tools?
- What mobile apps do you find most useful for work?

Mobile apps that may easily sync with desktop applications are great conversation starters within the context of the first stages of an embedded librarian plan. What tools are being used and why they are preferred are popular topics that help bridge the gap between the librarian and an outside partner. Discussing collaborative productivity tools that permit sharing and editing easily is a good way to introduce not only your expertise, but also to learn more about the inner operations of the organization you hope to embed. Therefore, talking about technology tools and also knowing how to use them are important parts for any embedded action plan.

⊚ Combining Information Services with Technology Tool Expertise

Earlier discussions in this chapter included using technology tools to work beyond library walls and needed technology expertise. Combining skills used in information services delivery with tech tools are everyday job duties for librarianship. Librarians are skilled in bringing together people, technology, information resources, and services in a very unique way. These human contact skills naturally will position librarians in leadership roles once their value as an embedded partner is recognized. The collaborative nature of librarianship and the special assistance an embedded librarian provides in technology, evaluating information, instruction, and information retrieval makes partnerships with outside organizations attractive and useful for both sides of the embedded program. Following are example scenarios of how librarians shared their expertise in library services and technology to create high-demand embedded partnerships.

College Business Librarian Embedded in a Small-Business Plans Poster Project

Embedded librarians may work within academic departments to create new assignments to change the design of the curriculum. An instruction session with an embedded librarian was requested by a college business professor who assigned the class to create group small-business plans. Although the student groups used credible library sources for their plans, the assignment was not as successful as the professor had hoped. The business plans were poorly written and would not have been useful in a real-world situation. The embedded librarian and professor worked together to revise the learning outcomes for the following semester. A new group assignment required students to attend a library session that was team taught by the embedded partners. Student groups were assigned to write a business plan and create a poster. The poster would be developed as a marketing pitch for a bank loan department to raise capital for their businesses. The embedded librarian not only taught students how to use reliable library subscription business databases but also recommended freely available resources for statistics, regional business, and occupational outlook information. Collaborative software such as shared database folders, slides, and documents were introduced as well as freely available poster creation instructions. The librarian assisted by working with the college printing office to send and print the posters at no charge. The class professor was introduced by the embedded librarian to key facilities process owners who assisted with scheduling the class posters and advertising the event. During the event, several professors were recruited by the librarian and professor to act as bank officers, selecting groups who would theoretically receive funding for their businesses. They would adjudicate the posters and award first-, second-, and third-place poster winners. The librarian helped organize the event, and the other professors involved in the event asked the librarian to provide more instruction within the business department courses the following semester.

Public Librarian Embedded in a Local Red Cross Office

A librarian working at a public library reference desk was asked for assistance in learning how to use a newly acquired hotspot by a patron. The librarian asked many open-ended questions during the reference interview and learned that the patron led the training at the local Red Cross office for disaster planning. A lively discussion ensued about how to deal with the problems of connectivity during a weather emergency. The librarian had knowledge of how social media was recently used by a local public library during a hurricane on the Gulf Coast and shared this information. The Red Cross administrator and librarian decided to embed the librarian within the staff disaster training at the local office, which resulted in the librarian creating a brief course designed to show how libraries may support responding agencies during a disaster.

School Librarian Embedded in an Open Educational Resources Grant

A group of high school mathematics teachers within a school district who were dissatisfied with the test scores in math for their students applied for and won a grant that would fund open educational resources (OERs), including software, for mathematics. The school administration was fully supportive of their work within the grant, but the teachers began to feel overwhelmed as they started to vet both the curriculum content and software available as OERs.

Although none of these teachers had much interaction with the school librarian, one of the teachers knew about the school librarian's work with using free education technology tools and OERs during various faculty development meetings. The librarian was invited to serve on the committee, and the teachers were pleased to discover the librarian's expertise in evaluating technology tools and helping select criteria, which made him a vital member of the grant team. The embedded librarian worked within the team to create an OER checklist for selecting both content and technology requirements needed to make the grant a success. Teachers were also introduced to using shared calendars and spreadsheets to help with managing the time spent on the grant project by the librarian. The embedded librarian assumed a leadership role for project management and technology tools.

Health Sciences Librarian Embedded in Clinical Pharmacology Rotations

A health sciences librarian who was embedded in both the optometry and pharmacy programs at a university stopped by the university drug information center to ask for information in order to assist an optometry student with a drug searching strategy. The drug information center was staffed by pharmacy students who were assigned to clinical rotations in their final year. The librarian was surprised to see a student attempt to use Google to answer a question (unsuccessfully) about a compounded drug solution for eyes. After much fact-finding with the faculty in charge of the drug center, the librarian created a LibGuide for clinical rotations, which included both library subscription databases with their corresponding mobile apps, as well as freely available drug information resources for after graduation. The librarian was invited as a guest lecturer at the beginning of the fourth-year clinical rotations to train students in using this LibGuide. The librarian was also invited to be embedded within the semi-annual pharmacy school mission in Jamaica, where she assisted with the creation of a shared barcoding system using free tech tools to track how drugs were used in the mission clinic as well as track how often a pharmacy student found it necessary to intervene to prevent drug interactions.

Academic Librarian Embedded in a Department's Promotion and Tenure Committee

A faculty member of a chemistry department's promotion and tenure committee called a librarian who had assisted her earlier in the semester with a research project. The professor was seeking information about open access journals, bibliometrics, and whether the criteria used for promotion and tenure should change due to the emergence of open access publishers, especially for new faculty from outside the United States. The librarian was invited to give a presentation at the next departmental meeting about open access versus traditional publishing models, citation metrics, and how to learn more about changing publishing models. The workshop was successful, and the librarian was invited to join the department's promotion and tenure committee. The librarian actively worked as an embedded committee member to help benchmark tenure standards and serve as a resource for the committee. The open access workshop became a part of faculty development programs used at the health professions division at the university.

Embedded Librarians and Medical Informatics

The evolving field of medical informatics education within the various health professions provides an interesting overlap for embedded librarian tech skills and information science knowledge. A 2013 survey of the role of librarians in informatics education demonstrated embedded librarian leaders who made significant contributions. The information skills of librarians were found to "provide relevance beyond their traditional roles" (King and Lapidus, 2015: 17).

⑥ Developing the Expert Embedded Librarian Professional Identity

All these examples illustrate how valuable an embedded librarian can be in various institutions. The expected technology skill set for librarians, plus the collaborative nature of librarianship, help embedded librarians work well within outside teams. Mindful development of these skills in technology and collaboration are important tools to use in an embedded librarian's action plan. These competencies, mixed with skilled reference interview techniques, strong searching, and information retrieval skills, are winning combinations that librarians should continue to work on improving. Library leaders who help develop group and teamwork abilities for librarians and allow time for librarians to learn to use new tech tools will find well-prepared librarians for any embedded librarian program.

The impact of the embedded program on the librarian's professional identity is indelible and will also affect both the physical spaces within the library and the technologies within the virtual spaces. The examples listed by library type above illustrate the unique services that may be provided using the embedded librarian's expert assistance as a resource and technology leader. Many librarians describe these embedded experiences as transformational (Linton, 2016). According to Linton's article on emerging roles, embedded librarians may observe a need for new library services, technologies, and platforms as well as new library spaces, better aligned with institutional or educational goals. Embedded librarians may find themselves leading technology initiatives within the library as "more of an educator than a librarian" (2016: 427). The librarian will also begin to see the importance of moving from a supporting role to a true embedded partner.

Embedded librarians may also find that their expertise in connecting people to technology and to other people and making "change happen through people" (Sullo and Gomes, 2016: 156) creates new leadership opportunities. Because embedded librarians work with outside groups, they may come to view the usability of library resources and user experiences with library technology with a new, more neutral perspective. The librarian will be able to share the unique user's point of view of the library gained by using library services and resources to assist the embedded group with their information needs. Interaction with the embedded librarian increases engagement with all the library offers—library instruction, interlibrary loan, vast online resources, instructional tools, and more. The willingness of embedded librarians to use their expertise in bringing together interdisciplinary technology interests to share ideas helps to increase the visibility of library services and resources. The organizational skills and knowledge of potential cross-disciplinary partner interests make embedded librarians attractive partners and position them as leaders in technology and information services.

This chapter has outlined clearly how embedded librarians are poised to step into leadership roles in both technology as well as the applications of technology to various subject areas. Embedded librarians bring traditional librarian technology and information services within outside organizations, using their expertise to forge new emerging leadership roles. These librarians also learn critical informational needs about the embedded group, allowing new insights into improving technology and library services for users. The librarian has a tremendous opportunity to share information services expertise, learn about the embedded group's needs and challenges, and serve as a leader to develop new technology tools and library services.

Key Points

Embedded librarians work beyond library walls and discover leadership opportunities within embedded organizations. Technology proficiencies and the librarian perspective increase the demand for embedded librarian services. Here are some important things to remember:

- Using the traditional librarian skill sets for technology translates well into technology leadership within the embedded organization.
- Working efficiently beyond the library walls is possible with tech tools and resolves time management or communication challenges for embedded librarians.
- Learning to use course management platforms, and virtual communication and meeting tools, may result in technology leadership opportunities within the embedded organization and the library.
- Bringing people together using technology and providing expert information services creates leadership roles for embedded librarians, transforming them into strong working partners and increasing the visibility of the library.

Embedded librarians make excellent leaders who make significant contributions to embedded groups. Their technology skills and traditional librarian values of access and intellectual freedom bring cognitive diversity into embedded groups. The next chapter will discuss hallmarks of successfully embedded programs and empower the reader to take the next steps into embedded librarianship.

References

Braun, Linda W. 2016. "Using Design Thinking: Providing a Framework for Youth Activities." *American Libraries* 47, no. 6: 80. https://americanlibrariesmagazine.org/2016/05/31/using-design-thinking/.

Clifton, Shari, and Phill Jo. 2016. "A Journey Worth Taking: Exploring a Hybrid Embedded Library Instruction Model through Three Distinct Cases." *Medical References Quarterly* 35, no. 3: 305–18. https://www.tandfonline.com/doi/full/10.1080/02763869.2016.1189784.

Duke University Libraries. 2018. "Crazy Smart / Personal Librarian Program." *Duke University Libraries Residence Hall Librarian Program.* https://library.duke.edu/residence-hall-librarian.

Edudemic.com. 2017. "The Teacher's Guide to Flipped Classroom." *The Teacher's Guides to Learning and Technology.* http://www.edudemic.com/guides/flipped-classrooms-guide/.

Fenton, William. 2018. "The Best (LMS) Learning Management Systems for 2018." *PC Magazine.* https://www.pcmag.com/article2/0,2817,2488347,00.asp.

Garcia-Milian, Rolando, Hannah F. Norton, Beth Auten, Valrie I. Davis, Kristi L. Holmes, Margeaux Johnson, and Michele R. Tennant. 2013. "Librarians as Part of Cross-Disciplinary, Multi-institutional Team Projects: Experiences from the VIVO Collaboration." *Science and Technology Libraries* 32, no. 2: 160–75. https://www.ncbi.nlm.nih.gov/pmc/articles/PMC3700548/#.

King, Samuel B., and Mariana Lapidus. 2015. "*Metropolis* Revisited: The Evolving Role of Librarians in Informatics Education for the Health Professions." *Journal of the Medical Library Association* 103, no. 1 (January): 14–18. https://www.ncbi.nlm.nih.gov/pmc/articles/PMC4279927/.

Linton, Anne M. 2016. "Emerging Roles for Librarians in the Medical School Curriculum and the Impact on Professional Identity." *Medical Reference Services Quarterly* 35, no. 4 (October–December): 414–33. https://www.tandfonline.com/doi/full/10.1080/02763869.2016.1220758.

Martinez, Juan, and Molly K. McLaughlin. 2017. "The Best Video Conferencing Software of 2017." *PC Magazine Reviews*, August 30, 2017. https://www.pcmag.com/article2/0,2817,2388678,00.asp.

Nagarkar, Shubhada, and Durga Murari. 2010. "Embedded Librarian: A New Role for Library and Information Professionals." Proceedings of the National Conference on Empowering Library Professional in Managing the Digital Resources and Providing Extension Activities, St. Agnes College, Mangalore. *ResearchGate*. https://www.researchgate.net/publication/304276194_EMBEDDED_LIBRARIAN_a_new_role_for_library_and_Information_professionals.

Quality Matters. 2014. "Course Design Rubric Standards." *QM Rubrics and Standards, Higher Ed Design Rubric.* https://www.qualitymatters.org/qa-resources/rubric-standards/higher-ed-rubric.

Schulte, Stephanie J. 2012. "Embedded Academic Librarianship: A Review of the Literature." *Evidence Based Library and Information Practice* 7, no. 4: 122–38. https://doi.org/10.18438/B8M60D.

Smith, Dave. 2017. "Top Collaboration and Communication Tools for the Digital Workplace." *DocumentStrategy*, December 20, 2017. DocumentMedia.com. http://documentmedia.com/article-2754-Top-Collaboration-and-Communication-Tools-for-the-Digital-Workplace.html.

Sullo, Elaine, and Alexandra W. Gomes. 2016. "A Profession without Limits: The Changing Role of Reference Librarians." *Medical Reference Services Quarterly* 35, no. 2: 145–57. https://www.tandfonline.com/doi/abs/10.1080/02763869.2016.1152141.

Thomas, Elizabeth A., and Anne McIntosh. 2013. "Embedded Librarianship: A Collaboration That Improves Student Learning Outcomes." *The League for Innovation in the Community College* 8, no. 10 (October). https://www.league.org/innovation-showcase/embedded-librarianship-collaboration-improves-student-learning-outcomes.

⑥ Further Reading

Kubelka, Morgan. 2016. "Partnering for Success: Best Practices in Embedded Librarianship." *Discover the Future of Research*, Wiley Network blog. November 9, 2016. https://hub.wiley.com/community/exchanges/discover/blog/2016/11/08/partnering-for-success-best-practices-in-embedded-librarianship.

Lemley, Trey. 2016. "Virtual Embedded Librarianship Program: A Personal View." *Journal of the Medical Library Association* 104, no. 3 (July): 232–34. https://doi.org/10.3163/1536-5050.104.3.010.

Rosenberg, Rachel. 2016. "Embedded Librarians Support Faculty, Students Where They Work." *University of Chicago Library News*, October 25, 2016. http://news.lib.uchicago.edu/blog/2016/10/25/embedded-librarians-support-faculty-students-where-they-work/.

Skiba, Diane J. 2017. "Quality Standards for Online Learning." *Nursing Education Perspectives* 38, no. 6 (November/December): 364–65. https://journals.lww.com/neponline/Fulltext/2017/11000/Quality_Standards_for_Online_Learning.21.aspx.

CHAPTER 10

The Empowered and Successful Embedded Librarian

IN THIS CHAPTER

▷ Managing the impact of the embedded program on library staff and services

▷ Evaluating the impact of the embedded librarian role

▷ Operating as an advocate for embedded librarianship

▷ Empowering the embedded librarian

HALLMARKS FOR ANY SUCCESSFUL PROGRAM share common components such as careful project management, measurable goal setting, and tracking the allotted budget. An embedded librarian initiative requires additional preparations as a successful program will affect library staff, resources, and funding. Another strong indicator of a successful embedded program is a busier library due to a new awareness of library services from the embedded group. Embedded librarians carry individual expertise as well as the talents and resources from the library they represent. They serve as advocates for supporting and funding libraries. Their actions illustrate the strong contributions that librarians bring to communities. This chapter brings together final points to assist in creating an empowered, successful embedded program.

Managing the Impact of the Embedded Librarian Program

Earlier chapters have discussed researching organizations to plan for embedded programs, performing SWOT analyses, and the importance of goal setting. An organized embedded program also requires initial preparations at the library to ensure success, a confident approach, and library staff support. The onset for the initiative may include staff training, setting up staff feedback and sharing methods, and tracking library team progress. The use of tech tools will help later with maintaining the program as well.

Library Services Impacted

The embedded librarian depends on library staff services and excellence in customer service skills to carry out library services promised to an embedded organization. Setting a goal for working as a team includes careful staff training and sharing outcomes for the embedded program. Heightened awareness and visibility of the library within the embedded group will impact staff workload. The library will most likely experience an increased demand for services as the embedded librarian begins outreach and working with the outside organization. Public service desks will see an increase in statistics. Other librarians who may not initially envision themselves as part of the embedded program may see an increased workload due to greater awareness or usage of the services that librarians offer. Staff working at public service desks will see an increase in checkouts of materials, more questions and requests for assistance. If the library is an academic or school library, instruction requests may increase dramatically. Research and medical libraries may see more faculty requests for interlibrary loans. Staff working at a public library may experience added programming responsibilities, larger enrollment in library classes or at library events, and more purchase requests. If the librarian is a solo librarian, increased patron interest in the library may be difficult to juggle without proper planning.

LIBRARY SERVICES IMPACTED BY EMBEDDED PROGRAMS

Types of library services that may be expected to increase as a result of an embedded librarian program include:

- Online chat utilization
- Interlibrary loan/document delivery requests
- Circulation services
- Purchase requests
- Collection usage
- Library website hits
- Tutorial and instruction tool usage

Library Staff Preparations for the Impact of the Embedded Program

Sustainable embedded librarian programs use data analysis to drive their efforts. Managing the impact of the program will require library staff to take a new look at the types of statistics currently collected—including outcomes—and review training on data management. Training for tracking library services will help staff understand their roles and responsibilities within the embedded librarian program. Proper assessment tools and interpretation of outcomes will aid in staffing, resource allocation, and justification for the program.

Following is a list of requested services provided by embedded or non-embedded librarians, which may be expected to increase as a result of an academic embedded librarian program:

- Instruction sessions—in both embedded and non-embedded programs
- Instructive reference interactions—especially virtual chat or email
- Faculty or student group outreach presentation requests
- Creation requests for instruction tools such as class guides (LibGuides)
- Informal reference questions within the embedded environment

Embedded librarian programs highlight and promote library services, especially those provided by librarians. Non-embedded librarians will be affected by an increased demand for instruction and faculty interaction. All librarians may find themselves more involved in institutional or community initiatives. This impact may be managed by creating virtual tools such as LibGuides that may be used for virtual instruction or outreach purposes. Expanded visibility may create new opportunities for librarians not yet embedded in outside organizations.

Collecting Embedded Reference Transactions Data to Demonstrate Impact

An article by O'Toole, Barham, and Monahan (2016) discusses how librarian transactions at the University of North Texas increased after embedding librarians into several departments, including physically moving their offices into these spaces. Statistics over three semesters included pre-embedded and post-embedded semesters. The article states that reference and instruction interactions increased and acknowledged that numbers of casual faculty reference interactions were not always tracked. Although the librarians were embedded in different departments—art, biology, and education—all experienced an increased number of instruction and reference requests.

It is important to examine how well these casual reference transactions are classified and tracked. It provides justification to enable decision-making, such as confirming why an embedded librarian holds office hours within an outside department. Successful embedded programs collect data rather than depending on anecdotal evidence. Data tells a story that demonstrates impact. Creating learning outcomes that are easily defined for reference questions may be helpful for creating statistics that describe these encounters. Training for writing these outcomes may be needed to guide embedded statistics collection.

Traditional reference transaction accounting counts the number of questions, classifying them as either directional ("Where is X?" "Does the library checkout X?")—or as reference questions ("I need help finding articles about X"). This type information is typically recorded in national reporting surveys for libraries. The Association of Research Libraries' (ARL) annual survey includes the number of reference transactions but does not include data that describes the details of these services (ARL, 2017). Current statistical methods may need revision for the embedded program. Rather than counting only how many questions are answered, the librarian may want to develop a classification system to analyze and quantify the types of assistance provided. Learning outcomes met through librarian assistance are easy to track, and cultural gaps in information-seeking behavior may help the embedded librarian find ways to focus efforts to work smarter.

SAMPLE LEARNING OUTCOMES FOR EMBEDDED REFERENCE QUESTIONS

Learning outcomes should be easy to understand and applicable to the types of questions asked within the embedded environment, and the method for collection should be simple to use. Here are some examples of learning outcomes for use by an embedded academic librarian:

"Following a reference interview with an expert librarian, faculty/students will be able to . . .

- Locate e-resources relevant to a topic using library databases and their search tools
- Plan a search strategy using keywords and appropriate sources
- Use criteria to evaluate the currency, relevancy, author, accuracy, purpose (audience) of a source, and/or determine its rhetorical value"

(Mlinar, 2017)

Embedded librarian reference learning outcomes tracking will help communicate the impact of the librarian and program, especially in demonstrating frequency of requests for assistance. It will show the embedded librarian's involvement in the curriculum, research, and daily lives of faculty. A health sciences professor may stop the embedded librarian in the hallway to ask for help in creating a class research poster assignment. A city planning committee chair may turn to a librarian during a meeting and ask for assistance in researching/benchmarking similar city initiatives. A school librarian embedded within a curriculum committee may be asked about library resources or databases that may replace textbooks. Tracking outcomes from these questions demonstrates the need for and impact of the embedded librarian within these institutional environments.

It is also important to use the language of the embedded department when reporting in order to show value-added services in the embedded librarian transaction. If jargon is used in writing outcomes, it should be from the embedded organization, not library jargon. For example, topic development assistance for a health sciences department may include a discussion about patient care plans, medication differential diagnosis, or complementary medicine.

According to Kloda and Bartlett (2013), the same clinical question formulation structure first developed by Richardson et al. in 1995, known by the acronym PICO (patient, intervention, comparison, and outcome), may be used to examine reference questions. Developing a framework for defining a reference question in a problem-solving context may be useful for effectively recording embedded reference data. The reference question about developing a topic may include a discussion about stakeholders, services, comparison, and desired results. An acronym tailored to the embedded group similar to the PICO acronym may be useful in formulating ways to track all the questions taken in the field. It is important for the embedded librarian to be trained in writing customizable learning outcomes in order to understand how to track these important elements within reference transactions.

⊚ Evaluating the Impact of the Embedded Librarian Role

The value of embedded librarian services is measurable and should be shared to demonstrate the importance of this role within the embedded community. It is critical to plan how data will be tracked using technology that is simple to use. Once the embedded librarian begins to work within the outside group, these statistics will help evaluate embedded services and help focus efforts to maximize positive outcomes. Regular communications regarding embedded community accomplishments and the librarian's role in meeting these goals help to justify and expand the embedded librarian program. Data management that is shareable and understandable helps evaluate the role of the embedded librarian.

Using Shared Data Tools to Track Impact

Staff training and preparation is vital to the success of the program, and this important role within the library team must be emphasized. The embedded librarian promoting library services and resources depends on library staff delivering excellent customer service and meeting expectations of the embedded department. Creating tools to support the library team and sharing the editing of training materials as well as technology training for these tools will provide support for library staff in carrying out new and old duties within the embedded program. Shared documents will help communicate expectations and responsibilities to demonstrate library staff value.

Documenting increased library usage and new embedded services develops library staff teamwork. Embedded librarians point to needed library resources and services while answering questions and delivering instruction. The increased number of librarian consultations, instruction opportunities, and group presentations to embedded departments supports the value of the library and this embedded role (Blake et al., 2016).

Document sharing tools with editing rights are powerful instruments for creating consistency and unifying library staff. It is important to find tools that are available in a variety of interoperable formats such as desktop, tablet, and mobile applications (apps) to set up ease of use and portability. For example, an internal wiki may be used to create scripts, post new program developments, and develop new team-based policies and procedures. Both free and paid options for creating a wiki are available, and many require very minimal training. A wiki may be divided into workspaces to selectively share information with the outside embedded organization. Workspaces may be used to identify embedded services and process owner partnerships. The embedded librarian may use the wiki to develop and share goals so that both library staff and embedded outside partners may communicate and manage workload responsibilities.

Parts of the wiki may be used internally—solely for managing embedded librarian impact on library staff. There are many examples of content that would be useful to add to an internal wiki. The embedded librarian may share key contacts from the embedded organization with instructions and follow-up information. As staff encounters questions for new situations, prescriptive procedures or suggested sample scripts may be added. Scripts may be included in staff training to practice role-playing situations and to thoroughly prepare staff for new transactions.

RECOMMENDED DOCUMENT SHARING TOOLS

It is recommended to have an assortment of sharing tool types to use. Some tools allow synchronous editing while others include the ability to upload files. Here is a list with some examples for use:

- Wiki: scripts, processes, procedures, goals
- Google Docs, Sheets, Slides: synchronous and asynchronous works, data tracking
- Internal LibGuides: shared forms, announcements, data sharing

USING SCRIPTS TO GUIDE STAFF INTERACTIONS WITH EMBEDDED PATRONS

New scripts must be dynamic, allowing for staff feedback and revisions. A script created in advance may need to be improved as it is put into practice. Staff permissions to edit, revise, or create new scripts as needed is an important part of the process. Scripts may serve as examples that would help staff to handle challenging situations. Any script could be modified or updated by other staff to work in a variety of patron encounters. Non-embedded librarians may use them to follow up with patrons from the embedded group. Examples for scripts for non-embedded librarian use include:

- Faculty looking for a library resource that has been discontinued such as a database or old material format (VHS) and recently replaced as part of the embedded partnership
- Instruction requests not related to specific research assignments (requests for tours), which may occur when faculty adjacent to the embedded department learn about available instruction
- Faculty seeking materials replaced by request from their embedded department with updated resources

Scripts for circulation staff may include questions for embedded and non-embedded patrons about course reserves, damaged items, or disruptive patrons. The collective wisdom used to create shared scripts and their variations is vital to cohesive communication, consistent customer services, and teamwork. Staff from diverse skill levels should be encouraged to contribute feedback and be included in the embedded program's success. Some libraries also adapt Google applications such as Google Docs, and others use password-protected LibGuides for this purpose. These tools promote transparent communication and consistency.

It is important that library staff participate in creating script or training content, not only due to their expertise but also to feel a sense of control over the changes they may experience during the embedded program's implementation. Workers who can envision their roles within the program gain more job satisfaction, ownership, and confidence in helping carry out the goals for the program. As the library becomes busier, staff will experience more pride in their work as well as in the library, seeing firsthand the fruits of their efforts. It is also probable that some library services that were not regularly used in the past may be requested. Library staff may need refresher instruction and training on providing these services, such as interlibrary loan or state book borrowing programs, especially if procedures used for the embedded department differ from those used in the past. If the embedded librarian is a solo librarian or has a smaller staff, similar shared internal tools with administrators or stakeholders may be used to communicate new processes. For example, a solo school librarian may share documents with the school principal as well as the librarian's supervisor within the school district. Sharing documents helps keep these key players in the loop, especially if additional funding or duties need to be discussed. The librarian may need to provide training for these tools for both staff who report to the librarian as well as those to whom the librarian reports. Transparency and visibility will help the librarian garner needed support to implement the embedded program. Solo librarians may also want to use more visual information in reporting the embedded program progress to stakeholders, to avoid excessive use of library jargon and illustrate successes within the program. For example, a list of contacts may be color-coded to indicate how many contacts have joined the embedded program. Also, a shared calendar color-coded to indicate embedded work time may help with communicating with stakeholders.

The embedded librarian will maximize success by keeping all stakeholders informed. Shared internal documents need to be updated frequently, and staff needs to understand how important timely communication can be to all involved. An organizational chart of the embedded organization that includes specific library services or resources associated with each person will help library staff provide better services to support embedded projects such as making library displays or adding simple signage.

SCENARIO: SHARED TOOLS—PUBLIC LIBRARIAN EMBEDDED IN CHARTER SCHOOL

Shared tools can be useful in developing new processes needed to support an embedded librarian program. A librarian working at a public library may plan to embed a charter middle school next door to the library. Library services offered may include information literacy instruction, reference help, and reading program support. Problems that may arise include:

- New procedures for issuing library cards to minors
- New rules about unattended minors in the library
- New processes for internet access and the availability of Wi-Fi

Shared documents may be used for library staff to discuss ideas for new processes and procedures. Once responses to these questions have been discussed, library staff may want to create scripts within the internal shared documentation to inform everyone how to proceed. The librarian must be careful to be inclusive of other staff at the library in sharing the progress of the embedded program and mindful of the possibility of increasing the workloads of others. Taking time to show gratitude for staff efforts and confirm their role in the embedded program success is very important.

Training may help with anticipating patron needs, but the shared documents may also help with communicating between the staff and the embedded librarian as to what services were actually requested. If staff are adequately prepared to be the expert at the desk, the quality of assistance is elevated and the patron experiences professional and competent help. The library team will share enthusiasm about the embedded librarian program and understand their strengths as they perform within the embedded team.

Managing the Impact on Library Services

Fitting the embedded librarian program within the scope of library services may require creative use of technology or staffing solutions as well as planning to request more funding. Staff involvement in problem solving is also helpful to avoid going over budget. Adding embedded librarian services will bring many positive changes such as increased library usage and a busier work environment. Staff ownership in the embedded librarian program will also increase morale and collegiality.

Library services provided by the embedded librarian are customized to group needs and goals. The librarian not only points embedded partners to library resources, but also concentrates on how library services may be used to help resolve problems faced by the embedded organization. Library services will be used as new tools by the embedded group. Library staff may find themselves offering library services within unfamiliar contexts or formats. Staff and services performed by library staff may directly affect research, teaching, or other work performed by the embedded partners (Vijesh, Anitha, and Rehana, 2017).

Maintaining the embedded librarian program within the current library budget should be communicated as a shared staff goal. New problems will arise, and staff may provide administrators with a wealth of creative solutions that will not require additional funding. Gathering and meticulously recording embedded program statistics that show both growth and patron benefits will create data that can be used for future budget planning. Organized metadata will provide the library team with evidence to use in considering the sustainability of the program. Data-driven decisions help with future budget requests or funding library staffing and resources to support the embedded librarian program. The embedded librarian program will increase the visibility of the library, especially to those involved in reaping the benefits of participation in the program. This added visibility may create new partners in budget planning and advocacy for continuing library services to this group.

Operating as an Advocate for Embedded Librarianship

Advocacy for embedded librarianship communicates its value to stakeholders and the embedded organization. Effective promotion for an embedded librarian program includes sharing contextual data and networking. Advocacy connects other outside organizations who need the expertise of an embedded librarian within their circles. Sharing meaningful data demonstrates how librarians help embedded groups resolve challenges and reach important goals.

Success Indicators

Both qualitative and quantitative data may be used to track the success of the embedded librarian program. The most common success indicators for all types of embedded librarians include a measurable increase in library services usage, questions, and increased staff workloads as mentioned earlier. For this reason, proper planning and setting up tools to track these indicators is essential, along with staff training plus cross-training in recording data. Embedded librarians or library administrators will need to inventory what data is currently being captured and plan for recording and comparing new and additional data.

Librarians who are embedded within academic departments or individual courses may want to find ways to collect data that not only counts transactions (number of instruction sessions, instructive reference transactions) but also communicates the value of the embedded academic librarian role. It is important to create data points that track embedded librarian services for situating information literacy within courses. Showing how the embedded librarian transforms a learning community is powerful and a great advocacy tool. Gathering feedback before and after an embedded librarian joins the community is important. For example, if a librarian plans to embed him- or herself within the English department at a university, it would be useful to find what data already exists. This would include library instruction sessions for that department, collection development data, database usage, print collection checkouts, interlibrary loan for this department, and what percentage of the department is already working closely with the library to use as baseline statistics. This information will serve as a starting point to indicate the impact of the embedded librarian program.

Using Embedded and Non-embedded Data for Advocacy

Library staff must be cross-trained to deal with and record all types of statistics collected. Crunching consistent numbers that indicate library impact within the community will affect everyone involved. Mindfulness of the format in which statistics are gathered will contribute to the team effort in supporting the embedded librarian.

The most common embedded librarian programs in higher education work within departments who require research assignments as a part of the academic curriculum. Subject areas include English, history, humanities, speech, communications, journalism, and courses that are writing intensive. An English department may require students within an entry-level course to write an informational paper and a persuasive essay, requiring student research using library resources and provide citations. The embedded librarian may be listed as guest lecturer, teach more than once per semester, be embedded within the course management system, and provide instructional tools such as a "Choosing a Topic" tutorial or class LibGuides. Examples of statistics related to library instruction within the example above of an embedded English department include:

- Number of students receiving instruction
- Student learning outcomes addressed during the session
- Professor name, course number
- Usage of reserve items, handouts, tutorials, or course guides related to the instruction session
- Amount of preparation time for librarian for instruction sessions
- Assessment of learning
- Instructor evaluation tools used during an instruction session
- Name of librarian teaching the session
- Length of session
- Data about additional sessions within the same course

- Information about the instruction request—date, time, and so forth.
- Learning outcomes addressed
- Asynchronous instructional tools used
- Discussion forum online—data about interactions, learning outcomes

This data may be used to track how many sessions for the English department were taught within the semester, which courses had instruction, what percentage of students within a specific course number received an information literacy session, which professors are more embedded with the librarian than others, how many students within the college received information literacy instruction, and much more. Comparisons may be made between embedded and non-embedded courses. Data that indicates growth and student success is especially valuable for continuing an embedded librarian program. Linking data to the mission and goals of the institution such as retention, student academic success, and equity will advocate for the academic department, the library, and the embedded librarian program. Surveys of faculty detailing how well students performed on the related research assignment and self- or peer evaluations by students may also assist with evaluating the success of the embedded librarian instructional role.

Evidence-Based Advocacy

Embedded librarians in community programs have produced evidence for their impact—advocating for public libraries, embedded librarians, and the embedded community organization. Douglas County Libraries (DCL) began providing community reference assistance for local development councils in 2006. The public librarians provided expert research and became valued community partners. By 2010 a team of five embedded librarians working with a local economic development council provided extensive research help, including the creation, data management, and a full report from a community survey. The information was presented to the Castle Rock Economic Development Council and continues to be a frequently requested source of information to city officials, developers, and county groups. The DCL librarians began to embed more community groups as community leaders advocated their research expertise and partnerships. DCL began to track data from various projects to share with other embedded staff by creating a WordPress blog, and organizing and sharing information about embedded groups. Information gathered within the blog helps embedded librarians easily research what other groups are doing within the community to help embedded community groups make important connections on shared issues. The blog was used to coordinate and direct embedded librarian efforts for maximum impact within the community, demonstrating the value of library partnerships throughout the community (Galston et al., 2012).

Advocacy Challenges

Embedded librarianship focuses on relationships. Traditional library services focused on getting the right resources as needed. Seeing yourself as the expert and as the commodity may be challenging. The embedded librarian works to solve problems and adds value to the embedded community. It may be challenging to learn how to demonstrate value rather than count transactions. Operating as an advocate is included in the ACRL *Roles and Strengths of Teaching Librarians*, which revised the *Standards for Proficiencies for Instruction Librarians and Coordinators* in 2017. According to this new standard, the advocate "will need to be able to contextually situate information literacy and communicate its value across a wide range of audiences" (ACRL, 2017). Value may be demonstrated in a variety of ways including data, working as a partner within institutional initiatives, partnering with faculty or within the community, and taking a role in student or community development.

Not all embedded partnerships will be successful. Data that points to small failures may be used to determine what does not work within embedded communities. Other indicators not recorded as a normal part of librarian statistics may indicate areas needed for improvement within the embedded program, such as professors who drop out of the program unexpectedly. For example, a professor may request library instruction sessions for all course sections taught in the fall semester but makes no requests in the following semester. Conversation will be needed to find out if the professor is dissatisfied with the instruction session; content, instruction delivery, or other issues may need to be discussed. If the librarian is asked to create a LibGuide or tutorial for a course, but the professor stops assigning use of these tools in subsequent semesters, the librarian will need to meet with the professor and learn how to proceed. Not every effort will be rewarded, and feedback will help library staff adapt support to meet academic curricular needs. This feedback should also be recorded adjacent to regular instruction data.

Gathering Referrals Advocating for the Embedded Librarian Program

Surveys of both faculty and students may help gather both anecdotal and qualitative success indicators. Simple testimonials of students who appreciate the embedded librarian assistance within the class or faculty who find improved research paper grades may be used. Examples of success indicators may include quotes from students or faculty such as:

- Faculty

  ○ My students used better quality resources for their paper this semester than in past semesters.
  ○ Students are showing more expertise in citing their sources.
  ○ Students are using library resources more frequently in their papers.

- Students

  ○ I am beginning to have a better understanding of how to use citations in my research paper.
  ○ I am discovering the library has most of the resources I needed to complete this assignment.
  ○ The librarian helped me improve my searching to find exactly what I wanted to use in my research paper.

Satisfied faculty also will spread the word across their departments and college about the advantages of having a librarian embedded within their curriculum. These referrals with formal data collection indicating student learning improvement are important for demonstrating the impact of the program. The library may be asked to place an embedded librarian within other departments as these successes are shared. The library may also want to create opportunities for outreach by attending or presenting at campus-wide workshops and offering services to departments not yet embedded, using the testimonial data already collected. Successful efforts and continued demand will increase the visibility of the library within the organization and bring even more requests for similar embedded services.

Communicating Advocacy and the Embedded Librarian

A successful embedded librarian program readily demonstrates the value of libraries and increases community awareness of librarian expertise and library services. Libraries offer services relevant to the needs of the community, but library managers often fail to communicate successes or advocate for better awareness of how libraries serve these needs. Communication strategies must be developed to promote the embedded program. It is important to share the impact of an embedded librarian program to stakeholders as it is specifically tailored to meet the needs of embedded communities. Strategic promotion describing library-embedded community engagement will help support the embedded librarian and lead to greater library staff collaboration and ownership.

Embedded librarians can play a key role in advocating for the library by providing primary sources that document value. Well-placed promotions are also useful. Posting photos on social media, on community websites, and on library materials can tell the story about the role the library plays within its community.

ALA Advocacy University is a great resource. It outlines action steps that are very applicable for any embedded librarian; these steps may be used by embedded librarians, as follows:

1. "Involve"—Library staff ownership and involvement in demonstrating library value for the embedded organization can be a very positive outcome for the embedded librarian program.
2. "Teach"—Creating scripts for frontline public service desks to describe how the embedded librarian works with the outside organization and what library services are focused on the program is important.
3. "Inform"—Consider writing about the embedded librarian program in community news websites, professional association publications, and email distribution lists.
4. "Illustrate"—Post information about the embedded programs or tell the story of student success using bookmarks, posters, flyers, promo items with photos, and testimonials.
5. "Encourage"—Communicate with staff how the program is helping the community and encourage them to talk about the embedded librarian program at meetings and home.
6. "Enlist"—Ask the library champions within the embedded program to help the librarian meet more colleagues and serve as a center of influence for others.
7. "Listen"—Give program participants an outlet to share stories of how the embedded librarian helped them reach their goals. Develop a community of library advocates to add more voices outside the library.
8. "Brainstorm"—Give program participants and library staff opportunities to brainstorm more ideas for marketing the program and advocating for the value added to the community.
9. "Welcome"—Look at the library and its online presence with an objective eye to detail: Is it cluttered? Is it welcoming? Is it clean and does it provide a hospitable presence for users?

10. "Thank"—Express gratitude and give credit to everyone who contributes to the program's success.

(ALA Advocacy University, 2017)

There are many other resources that share ideas about promoting libraries, such as the Miami-Dade Public Library System document *Strategies to Create Awareness of Library Services* (Awareness, Advocacy and Marketing Working Group, 2014). Illustrating how libraries help users is a common denominator in marketing strategies. Data visualizations are great tools for communicating impact and advocating for embedded programs. Programs such as Tableau, used by Ohio State University Libraries, aid stakeholders in rapidly analyzing data and identifying value (Buhler, Lewellen, and Murphy, 2016). Visualization software provides dashboards to observe trends and changes affected by embedded programs. Images and colors may be used to graphically show value-added services, thus increasing awareness and advocating for the embedded librarian.

Advocacy for the embedded partnership demonstrates the importance of shared efforts to achieve community goals. An embedded librarian program within the first-year experience Beacon Scholars classes at the University of Utah affected student success. The embedded librarian participated in class activities and provided information literacy instruction. Students were connected to university resources, improving retention. New cohort programs were developed with the librarian partnership for diverse student populations to help navigate and understand what support services were available. The embedded librarian served as an advocate for Beacon Scholars to library services with data about technology access, skills, and needs. A new library laptop, hotspot, and extended checkout program were added to library services. The embedded librarian was also able to overcome a common barrier experienced by first-year students—intimidation about library services. Students within the cohort became comfortable with asking the librarian for assistance and learned how to use the library to help them with their academic and technology needs (Parker, 2017).

Library services have evolved over the past thirty years, but awareness of these changes is limited. Most librarians encounter this lack of awareness regularly—"I didn't know you offered that service" is a commonly heard statement, no matter what type of library is involved. Embedded librarian programs focus on relevant services and resources for use, tailoring them for program participants and providing specialized librarian expertise. What librarians do and how relevant these duties are to the needs of library patrons is unfortunately a well-kept secret in most communities.

Embedded Librarianship Advocacy and ALA Core Values

Advocacy for embedded librarianship follows the ALA *Core Values of Librarianship*, namely, education and lifelong learning, and social responsibility (ALA Council, 2014). The embedded librarian builds a community of practice within the outside group, sharing the importance of information literacy and learning within the context of the community. Efforts for critical problem solving and social justice issues within the community using great resources advocate for librarianship and library services.

An article by Wu and Thornton (2017) describes how embedded librarians have impacted the College of Pharmacy at the University of Tennessee Health Science Center. Embedding the librarian into the curriculum impacted research teams, patient counseling, and pharmacy student research skills for lifelong learning. Data collected within this embedded model of practice indicated improved patient outcomes and increased researching interest for lifelong learning within the pharmacy community.

Embedded librarians make excellent contributions in educating users about both the value of libraries and also the importance of using librarians as a resource. No matter what type of library embarks on the embedded librarian program, it will increase the awareness of how librarians can help and how library services and resources are needed.

Empowerment and the Embedded Librarian

The work involved in creating an embedded librarian program is rewarding and enjoyable. No matter how a personality is described—extroverted or introverted, loud or quiet, enthused or calm—any librarian can find success as an embedded librarian. Sharing expertise outside the library walls delights and encourages those within embedded communities. Librarians provide cognitive diversity in outside organizations and offer new perspectives on problem solving. No matter the size of the library budget and number of resources and services, expertise in locating both library and freely available resources is unparalleled in any other profession.

Librarians and information literacy instruction within communities is one of the most relevant and needed services as information dissemination continues to favor speed over accuracy. The ability to evaluate news stories for accuracy, social media for credibility, and publisher platforms for content quality will continue to be important and relevant in academic institutions, schools, hospitals, and the workplace. Information literacy and evaluating information will continue to be common student learning outcomes across disciplines of academic study. An embedded librarian with a thorough understanding of the information needs for the outside organization will be empowered to lead and advocate for the value of libraries and the expertise of librarians.

Key Points

Embedded librarian programs impact not only the communities in which they are embedded, but also library staff and services. Mindful management of this impact requires staff preparation, training, and support. The program cannot be successful without teamwork and communication. Embedded librarians must be prepared to share data that tells a story to stakeholders within the embedded group and the library. Data may be used to demonstrate the impact and value of the embedded librarian role within the program. Connecting data points will be helpful in evaluating the impact of the program and advocating for embedded librarianship. Important points were discussed for a successful embedded librarian:

- The impact of an embedded librarian program may be artfully managed with mindful planning, staff training, and shared communication using smart productivity tools.
- Shared data may be used to evaluate the impact and describe the value of the embedded librarian role within the outside organization. The embedded librarian operates as an advocate for the expertise of librarians and embedded librarianship.
- Working as an embedded librarian is empowering and follows core values of librarianship.

The cognitive diversity offered by embedded librarians positively impacts outside organizations. Building collaborative relationships within embedded groups creates new opportunities for librarian expertise. Embedded librarians continue to experience an increasing demand for their skills and knowledge. They connect embedded partners with the resources needed to accomplish great things together, experiencing strong job satisfaction. Embedded partnerships grow together, developing creative solutions to modern information challenges. Libraries who offer embedded librarian programs advocate for the continued need for library services in the information age. Embedded librarians are empowered to make a difference within transformative, embedded partnerships.

References

ACRL (Association of College and Research Libraries). 2017. *Roles and Strengths of Teaching Librarians.* American Library Association. April 28, 2017. http://www.ala.org/acrl/standards/teachinglibrarians.

ALA (American Library Association) Advocacy University. 2017. *Ten Action Steps for Frontline School Advocacy.* American Library Association. http://www.ala.org/advocacy/advleg/advocacy university/frontline_advocacy/frontline_school/ten.

ALA (American Library Association) Council. 2014. *Core Values of Librarianship.* American Library Association. http://www.ala.org/advocacy/intfreedom/corevalues.

ARL (Association of Research Libraries). 2017. "ARL Statistics: About New Measures." *ARL Statistics: Annual Library Statistics.* http://www.arlstatistics.org/about/new_measures.

Awareness, Advocacy and Marketing Working Group. 2014. *Strategies to Create Awareness of Library Services.* Mayor's Blue Ribbon Taskforce for the Miami-Dade Public Library System, 2014. http://www.miamidade.gov/mayor/library/Awareness-Advocacy-and-Marketing -Working-Group/AAM07%20Strategies%20to%20Create%20Awareness%20of%20 Library%20Services/AAM7%20Strategies%20to%20Create%20Awareness%20of%20 Library%20Services.pdf.

Blake, Lindsay, Darra Ballance, Kathy Davies, Julie K. Gaines, Kim Mears, Peter Shipman, Maryska Connolly-Brown, and Vicki Burchfield. 2016. "Patron Perception and Utilization of an Embedded Librarian Program." *Journal of the Medical Library Association* 104, no. 3 (July): 226–30. https://doi.org/10.3163/1536-5050.104.3.008.

Buhler, Jeremy, Rachel Lewellen, and Sarah Ann Murphy. 2016. "Tableau Unleashed: Visualizing Library Data." *Research Library Issues: A Report from ARL, CNI, and SPARC*, no. 288: 21–36. http://publications.arl.org/rli288.

Galston, Colbe, Elizabeth Kelsen Huber, Katherine Johnson, and Amy Long. 2012. "Community Reference: Making Libraries Indispensable in a New Way." *American Libraries* 43, no. 5/6 (May/June): 46–50. http://www.jstor.org/stable/23278094.

Kloda, Lorie A., and Joan C. Bartlett. 2013. "Formulating Answerable Questions: Question Negotiation in Evidence-Based Practice." *Journal of the Canadian Health Libraries* 34, no. 2: 55–60. https://doi.org/10.5596/c13-019.

Mlinar, Courtney. 2017. "Desk Stats Student Learning Outcomes." *Austin Community College Library Services Wiki: Instructive Reference Workspace.* https://docs.google.com/spreadsheets/ d/1gKYwmsXdXoJzdZh4wBbxHJhD_8fZGr72Dmf0MCCOTs4/edit?usp=sharing.

O'Toole, Erin, Rebecca Barham, and Jo Monahan. 2016. "The Impact of Physically Embedded Librarianship on Academic Departments." *portal: Libraries and the Academy* 16, no. 3: 529–56. https://doi.org/10.135/pla.2016.0032.

Parker, Adriana. 2017. "Academic Libraries and Vulnerable Student Populations: A New Model of Embedded Librarianship for First-Generation University Students." *Political Librarian* 3, no. 1. https://openscholarship.wustl.edu/pollib/vol3/iss1/9.

Richardson, W. Scott, Mark C. Wilson, Jim Nishikawa, and Robert S. A. Hayward. 1995. "The Well-Built Clinical Question: A Key to Evidence-Based Decisions." *ACP Journal Club* 123, no. 3: A12. https://acpjc.acponline.org/Content/123/3/issue/ACPJC-1995-123-3-A12.htm.

Vijesh, P. V., B. Anitha, and N. C. Rehana. 2017. "From Traditional to the Futuristic: A Paradigm Shift towards Embedded Librarianship." 12th International CALIBER-2017. http://ir.inflibnet.ac.in:8080/ir/bitstream/1944/2086/1/42.pdf.

Wu Lin, and Joel Thornton. 2017. "Experience, Challenges, and Opportunities of Being Fully Embedded in a User Group." *Medical Reference Services Quarterly* 36, no. 2: 138–49. https://doi.org/10.1080/02763869.2017.1293978.

⑥ Further Reading

Calkins, Kaijsa, and Cassandra Kvenild. 2014. *The Embedded Librarian's Cookbook.* Chicago: Association of College and Research Libraries.

Daugherty, Alice, and Michael F. Russo. 2013. *Embedded Librarianship: What Every Academic Librarian Should Know.* Santa Barbara, CA: ABC-CLIO.

Hamilton, Buffy J. 2012. *Embedded Librarianship: Tools and Practices.* Chicago: American Library Association.

Kvenild, Cassandra, and Kaijsa Calkins, eds. 2011. *Embedded Librarians: Moving beyond One-Shot Instruction.* Chicago: Association of College and Research Libraries.

Lankes, R. David. 2011. *The Atlas of New Librarianship.* Cambridge, MA: MIT Press.

Mulder, Megan, and Carolyn Jones. 2012. *Putting the Material in Materiality: The Embedded Special Collections Librarian.* Chicago: Association of College and Research Libraries.

Shumaker, David. 2012. *The Embedded Librarian: Innovative Strategies for Taking Knowledge Where It's Needed.* Medford, NJ: Information Today.

Tumbleson, Beth E., and John J. Burke. 2013. *Embedding Librarianship in Learning Management Systems: A How-to-Do-It Manual for Librarians.* Chicago: Neal-Schuman.

Index

About the Author

Courtney Mlinar has worked for Austin Community College (ACC) since 2013 as a head librarian (Elgin campus) and associate professor. She is a member of the ACC Library Services Leadership Team, serving on the Information Literacy Council, and the LibGuides administrator and copyright officer for ACC. She earned a master's degree in library science from Texas Woman's University, a bachelor's degree in music education and performance from Southern Methodist University, and a master's degree in clarinet performance from Texas Christian University. She has worked as an embedded academic and health sciences librarian and as an instructor for the Medical Library Association Continuing Education Clearinghouse and Library Juice Academy, teaching embedded librarianship courses.

Courtney has worked as an educator for thirty-five years in public schools and higher education. She recently served on the Association of College and Research Libraries (ACRL) Instruction Section Task Force, revising the 2007 *Standards for Proficiencies for Instruction Librarians and Coordinators*, and co-authoring the 2017 *Roles and Strengths of Teaching Librarians* (http://www.ala.org/acrl/standards/teachinglibrarians/). She is the author of the *Library Professional Development* blog (https://libprofdev.wordpress.com/).